香港藝術節委約及製作
Commissioned & produced by
the Hong Kong Arts Festival

重回凡間的凡人
An Ordinary Man

潘燦良 Poon Chan-leung

英文翻譯 張敏儀
English Translation Margaret Cheung

New Plays Selection books by:

www.musemag.hk

Foreword

There is a view that words on a page are like orphans, with no one to give them articulation and no defense against possible misreading.

This is not the intended fate of words written for the stage. They are meant to be framed in a carefully controlled environment, spoken skillfully by talented actors who have painstakingly prepared the delivery of every syllable for a receptive audience to achieve maximum effect.

While the words on the following pages will not truly come alive until these conditions are satisfied, I hope their potential is evident, even when stripped and orphaned on the page, awaiting your imagination - or the resources of a full production - to animate them.

This is the third year in which the Festival has commissioned, produced and published new works. The intention is not only a matter of record, but also to facilitate each work's progress from the first Festival production to other stagings and re-imaginings, as a resource to the artistic community in Hong Kong and elsewhere in the world. Even while celebrating the premiere, I look forward eagerly to future productions.

It is a great pleasure and privilege to be able to present these words to you. I am grateful to my talented and dedicated colleagues for making it possible. I would also like to thank the many artists who work with us to bring the Hong Kong Arts Festival to life each year.

Tisa Ho
Executive Director, Hong Kong Arts Festival

前言

有一種說法認為，紙上的文字就像孤兒，既無人解讀，亦無人為其可能引起的誤讀辯護。

舞台劇本卻不應落得如此命運，它們應享有一個如溫室般的理想環境，由具才華的演員經過多番經營，才向一群有心的觀眾宣之於口，以達到最佳效果。

在未有這些條件以前，這本書中的文字仍沒有完整的生命，但我希望讀者能感受到這些紙上孤兒的潛質，它們正等待你的想像力，或者製作資源來賦予它們生命力。

這是藝術節委約、製作和出版新劇作的第三年，我們的目的不單是作為一份紀錄，更希望這次的首演能為香港以至世界各地的藝術社群帶來更多的重演和改篇劇目。在慶祝首演之際，我更期待未來的演出。

能在這裡與您分享以上的話，我深感榮幸。感謝各位能幹又勤奮的同事，令這個計劃得以實現。我亦要向所有藝術家說聲謝謝，全賴你們的參與，才能成就每一年的香港藝術節。

何嘉坤
香港藝術節行政總監

playwright's notes

A friend's father passed away. I grieved. I saw myself in his misery – something I had once gone through. I thought, "If we are meant to face it, let it come". This is life.

The loss of my father gave birth to this ordinary story, which takes the form of a collection of seemingly everyday events. It is the same old story of birth, aging, illness, death – and of love and hate. And it is all far more vivid and dramatic in real life than on the stage. You can never beat reality.

This is an ordinary, typical story. My friends wanted to know what I hoped to inspire, to reflect or to change through my story. I asked in response: Is it only worthwhile if it turns worldly affairs, or so-called "fate", upside down? Some think that only when artists do their best to actualise "the impossible" can their art be regarded meaningful. But I am a more humble person. I carry with me the notion of "Do you have to try that hard?" and I question whether many of the things we consider "nothing" are truly worthless. For some people, merely lamenting the misfortunes and inevitabilities of life isn't exciting enough. Or maybe it is just a different way of thinking, just a different perspective. Perhaps we have to put our own marks on the yardstick. The important thing is to develop your own set of standards and live accordingly. Some believe they can alter nature; some deny the existence of natural laws; some curse nature for not following the course they desire. Very few truly accept that nature is within us. We need to keep that in mind to co-exist with nature.

The theatre endows me with the aesthetic sense to appreciate life's beauty – be it good or evil, pretty or grotesque. Although I have yet to achieve "beauty", my relatively insignificant interest in the arts suffices to enrich my life. After twenty years as an actor, I see this opportunity to take up the roles of directing and playwriting as a blessing, a chance encounter.

It is not appropriate for me to judge or define my own work. I just hope that there is beauty in it. Six billion people give birth to six billion stories. The culture and civilisation of our generation are all built upon these human stories.

What would I like my audience to take home? Whether they agree with the story's messages isn't my main concern. My greatest wish is that the audience will remember that tonight, within these two hours at this particular point in life, this particular group of actors made us think about what we will all experience in our respective lives. I would be content with that. It also reflects my greatest belief in the theatre.

I would like to express my gratitude for the support of every actor, designer and front- and back-stage crew member. It is your devotion that has made this belief in theatre come to life. I would also like to thank the teachers and friends who have given me their opinions and advice. Thank you!

編劇的話

一個朋友的父親離去了，令我即時沉重下來。感同身受，想到是「要我們面對的就讓它來吧」，這就是人生。

這個平凡故事的創作起源由自己的父親去世所引發，用疑似生活化的事件呈現，同樣是生老病死愛與恨，但在生活中的每一點滴，都要比台上的來得強烈，而且比真實生活的更戲劇性。你永遠也敵不過它。

一個平凡又一般的故事，朋友問我要它來喚醒甚麼，反思甚麼或讓人改變甚麼。我倒想問是否一定要扭轉所謂命運世事的「人或事」才算有價值呢？有些人相信極其力量去做出你的「不能」，才是值得要說的話。可我這個一向低調的人，抱著「駛唔駛咁大力」的信念又被形容為「無嘢」是否就沒有存在價值？只是說出「生命無奈」對某些人來說確實不「過癮」。但這可能只是因人而異的配合問題。或許，就是要把這把尺放出來讓人去自己刻劃上面的刻度。而重點是你認知了自己所定的刻度後，就要靠你自己去運用它來面對未來的生活。有人相信可扭轉自然，有人會逃避自然的存在。有人會指控這種自然不合他口味。也許甚少人會承認自然根本就存在而與自然共存。先認知再共存。

潘燦良
Poon Chan-leung

POON CHAN-LEUNG joined the Hong Kong Repertory Theatre as full-time actor upon graduation from The Hong Kong Academy for Performing Arts in 1991. He has performed in more than one hundred productions, including *I Have A Date With Spring*, *The Legend of the Mad Phoenix*, *Three Sisters*, *The Crucible*, *A Dream Like a Dream*, *Peach Blossom Fan*, and *The Importance of Being Earnest*. His recent work includes *Bun in the Cave*, *Communicating Doors*, *Dr. Faustus*, and *Le Dieu Du Carnage*. He was director of the play *Boxer*, and was a member of the script-writing and directing team, as well as an actor, for *Crossings*.

The Hong Kong Federation of Drama Societies awarded him Best Supporting Actor for *Black Elk Speaks* in 1995 and for *A Small Family Business* in 2005.

Poon's acting credits also include the movies *An Umbrella Story*, *The Legend of the Mad Phoenix* and *Love a la Zen*. For his performance as Tong Tik-sang in *The Legend of the Mad Phoenix*, he was nominated for Best Supporting Actor in 1997 at both the Golden Horse Awards and the Hong Kong Film Awards 1998.

In 2005, the Asian Cultural Council awarded him a Lee Hysan Foundation Fellowship to study drama in the U.S.

劇場工作給予我欣賞「人生」這份「美」的審美觸覺，不論是善與惡，美與醜。縱然並未達到「美」層次，但我從事戲劇工作，對藝術的興趣，也許只是一點點，已足以令我的生命多彩多姿。二十多年站在演員的位置，今次有幸給予我編與導的嘗試和超越，是我的幸運，來得是緣。

我不想批判，評價、指引或定性它，我只希望觀審它的美。六十億人就有六十億個故事，建構出每一個世代的生態，文化與文明，但這一切都建基於人。

希望觀眾看完會得到甚麼？這個故事中的意義或訊息他們接納與否其次。我最希望觀眾會記得曾經有一個晚上，你是在一個特定的時間和這個劇場的這一班人遇上，共聚過兩個小時，曾經分享過一些我們共同面對過的生命歷程。這已經足以令我感到滿足。這也是我對劇場的最大信念。

感謝每一位支持的演員，設計師和前後台工作人員。是你們的投入把這份對劇場的信念實現出來。還要感謝每一位給與我意見和提點的老師和朋友們。多謝！

畢業於香港演藝學院戲劇學院表演系，現為香港話劇團的主要演員，在學期間已多次獲頒傑出演員獎和獎學金。至今參演劇目逾百齣，演繹過不少本地原創劇和古今中外名劇。其中被受注目的角色及演出包括《南海十三郎》飾唐滌生、《家庭作孽》飾何必達、《如夢之夢》、《黑鹿開口了》、《凡尼亞舅舅》、《不可兒戲》及《藝術》。近期演出包括《暗戀桃花源》飾江濱柳、《敦煌‧流沙‧包》飾史無例、《2029追殺1989》飾倪甚錦、《魔鬼契約》飾浮士德及《豆泥戰爭》飾

Michel HOULLIE。亦曾參與《三人行》的編作及導演，與及導演《拳手》。

另外，潘燦良亦曾參演電影《人間有情》、《南海十三郎》及《愛情觀自在》，憑《南海十三郎》中唐滌生一角分別獲提名97年度台灣金馬獎及98年度香港電影金像獎之最佳男配角獎。在香港戲劇協會舉辦的頒獎禮中，亦多次被提名及獲得獎項。

2005年，潘燦良獲亞洲文化協會頒發利希慎基金獎助金Lee Hysan Foundation Fellowships前赴美國紐約進修戲劇。

《重回凡間的凡人》首演於39屆香港藝術節，
2011年3月11日，香港文化中心劇場
An Ordinary Man premiered at the Studio
Theatre, Hong Kong Cultural Centre,
11 March 2011, 39th Hong Kong Arts Festival

導演 Director/編劇 Playwright
潘燦良 Poon Chan-leung

形象及服裝設計 Costume / Image Designer
郭家賜 Kary Kwok

舞台設計 Set Designer
邵偉敏 Siu Wai-man

燈光設計 Lighting Designer
張國永 Leo Cheung

音響設計 Sound Designer
彭俊傑 Pang Chun-kit

製作經理 Production Manager
張向明 Cheung Heung-ming

監製 Producer
香港藝術節 Hong Kong Arts Festival

主演 Cast

張錦程 Cheung Kam-ching	黎志寬 Li Zhi Kuan
陳敏斌 Chan Man-bun	大口 Da Kou
司徒慧焯 Szeto Wai-cheuk	忠 / 殯儀館事務職員 Zhong / Funeral parlor employees
蘇玉華 So Yuk-wa	琪 / 郭瑤 Qi / Guo Yao
黃哲希 Wong Chit-hei	姐 Sister
何英瓊 He Ying Qing	母親 Mother

角色表 List of Characters

黎志寬，三十多歲
Li Zhi Kuan (Kuan) - 30s

大口，三十多歲，寬的朋友，中學同學
Da Kou (Da) - 30s, Kuan's friend, secondary school classmate

忠，三十多歲，寬的朋友，中學同學
Zhong - 30s, Kuan's friend, secondary school classmate

琪，約二十五歲，寬的女友，空中小姐
Qi - About 25, Kuan's girlfriend, flight attendant

姐，近四十歲，寬的家姐
Sister - About 40, Kuan's sister

媽，約六十多歲，寬的母親
Mother - 60s, Kuan's mother

殯儀館事務職員
Funeral parlor employees

郭瑤，近三十歲，寬的前女友
Guo Yao - About 30, Kuan's ex-girlfriend

Scenes

My father died, and returned to the mortal world!
Did he leave too early, or did he return too late?
He helped us rediscover our feelings and emotions towards our lives, our families,
with our lovers, our friends. He made us redefine the value of our existence.

Scene 1	Dream
Scene 2	Bus Station to Shenzhen/Sauna Shop
Scene 3	Qi's Home
Scene 4	Outside the Intensive Care Unit
Scene 5	Kuan's Mother's Home
Scene 6	The Corner of Some Bar
Scene 7	A Corner of the Funeral Parlor
Scene 8	Kuan's Mother's Home
Scene 9	A Corner in the Hospital
Scene 10	Qi's Home
Scene 11	Kuan's World
Scene 12	Da Kou's Home
Scene 13	In the Corner of a Park
Scene 14	Kuan's Mother's Home
Scene 15	A Popular Coffee House
Scene 16	Outside of Qi's Residence
Scene 17	Outside the Shenzhen Sauna Shop
Scene 18	Outside the Hospital/Hospital ward
Scene 19	Outside of Qi's Residence
Scene 20	Nursing Home/Hospital Ward
Scene 21	Epilogue

分場

父親去世，他回到凡間！是他先去還是他來得太遲？
他展開了少有關心過的情感觸碰，對生命、家庭、愛人、朋友和
存在價值重新定義。

第一場	夢境
第二場	巴士站/桑拿店
第三場	琪家中
第四場	深切治療病房外
第五場	寬媽的家
第六場	酒吧
第七場	殯儀館辦事處
第八場	寬家的飯廳
第九場	醫院
第十場	琪家中
第十一場	寬的世界
第十二場	大口家
第十三場	公園
第十四場	寬家中
第十五場	咖啡店
第十六場	琪家外
第十七場	桑拿店外
第十八場	醫院/病房
第十九場	街上
第二十場	靈養院/病房
第二十一場	尾聲

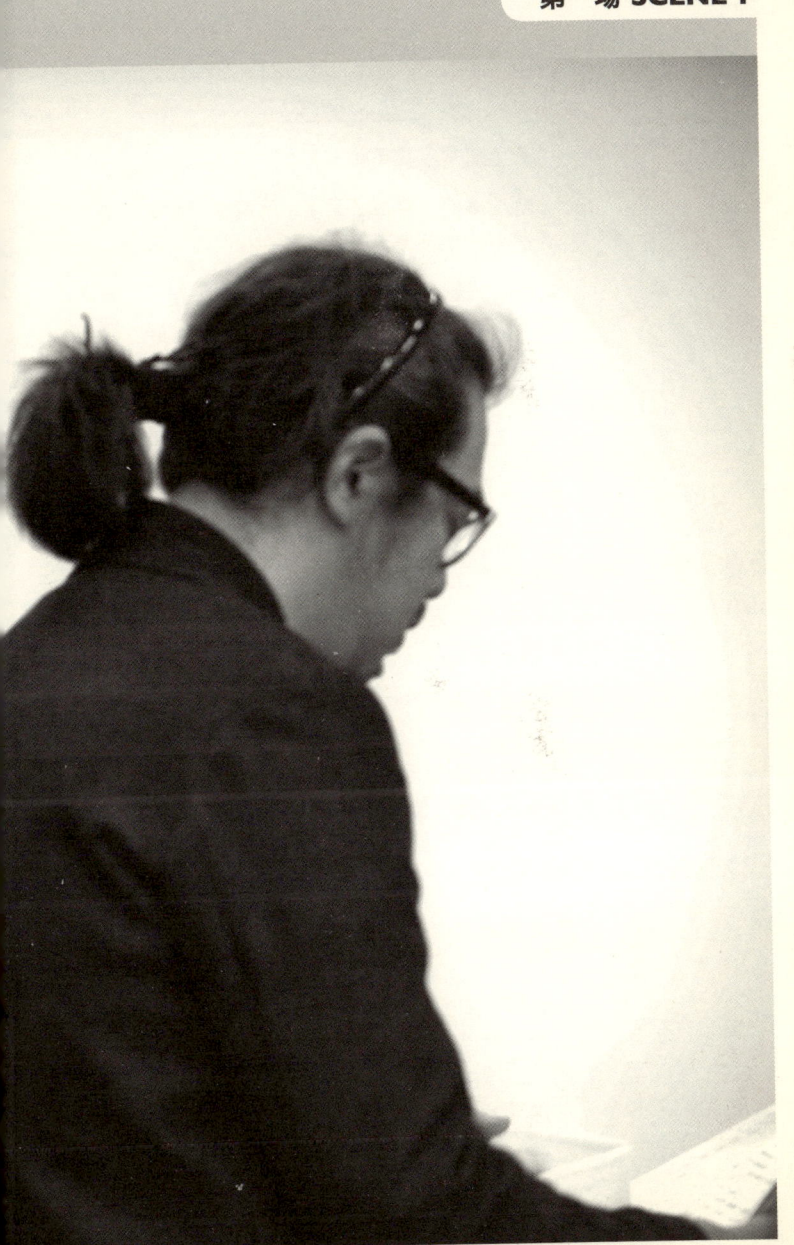

第一場：夢境

(*天上滿是星星閃爍。*)

(*燈光轉變，星星不見了，阿寬突然醒來，似是在夢中扎醒。*)

寬：　我發咗個夢，好似係去咗太空，(*一頓。*) 我浮咗喺太空度望返住個地球。四周圍好靜，靜到有啲得人驚，黑麻麻，但係有啲星星喺好遠度閃閃吓。突然間……我後面唔知有啲乜嘢……將我推埋去地球度。當我就嚟撞埋去嘅時候，個地球突然變咗做一個白色嘅枕頭，一個好大好大……地球咁大嘅白色枕頭。

我「啪」一聲撞咗埋去，雙手雙腳打開晒好似個大字咁 (*做出同樣的動作。*) 成個人全身每一吋都陷咗入去。郁唔倒又呀唔倒氣……成個人俾佢吞緊入去。

跟住個大枕頭開始穿過我身體……佢撐到我個口擘大咗……我想叫出嚟但係叫唔到……佢入咗我身體嘅每一「忽」，入咗我個口，然後經過喉嚨，落到個胃，填滿晒啲內臟……所有肌肉、細胞開始膨脹，手手腳腳都好似就嚟要爆咁。

就喺爆之前……「佢」穿過咗我，「就咁」穿透咗我。

跟住所有嘢都唔郁……變到好輕，我都變到好輕。唔係……係「空」咗……我好似空咗咁……不由自主咁維持喺失重嘅狀態，喺太空度漂浮。(*做出全身不能動彈的姿態。*)

好靜……我只係聽到自己心跳得好快……「迫仆……迫仆……迫仆」。

SCENE 1 – DREAM

(*Stars sparkle in the sky.*)

(*Lights change. Stars disappear. Kuan wakes suddenly, as if he was startled from his dream.*)

KUAN I had a dream. I think I was in outer space. (*A moment.*) I drifted in space as I watched the earth. It was quiet all around me. So quiet, it was scary. It was pitch black. But stars were sparkling in the distance. Suddenly… something behind me… pushed me towards the Earth. When I was just about to crash into the Earth, the Earth suddenly turned into a white pillow. A huge white pillow… as big as the earth. I fell into it with a big splat. My arms and legs were spread wide open. (*Makes the shape with his body.*) Every inch of my body sank into it. I couldn't move, I couldn't breathe… I was swallowed up. Then the huge pillow started to penetrate into me… It pushed itself into my mouth… I wanted to scream but I couldn't… It entered every part of my body. It went down my throat and into my stomach, filling every corner inside me… All my muscles, every cell, began to swell. My arms and legs felt like they would explode. Just before they were about to explode… "it" passed right through me. Like this. Then everything stopped moving… Everything became very light. I became very light. No… I mean, empty… I seemed empty…I was floating… floating in space. (*Puts his body into an unmovable shape.*) It was very quiet… I could only hear my heart beating very quickly… "boom boom… boom boom… boom boom.."

（一頓。）

你想大喊一場但係你會喊唔出聲……（*嘗試大叫，但只能輕輕「呀」了一聲。*）呀……！

（*稍頓。*）

我就醒咗……（*按著自己急速跳動的心口。*）呢個夢……間唔中都發一次……

（*電話響聲出現，寬有點呆。*）

（*忠和大口出現台上遠處。*）

忠： （*直接向寬*）阿寬！

（*緊接下場。*）

(*A moment.*)

You want to cry your heart out but you can't make a sound… (*Tries to scream but can only make a soft "Ah" sound.*) Ah…!

(*A moment.*)

I woke up… (*Holds onto his heart, which is beating quickly.*) This dream… I have it every once in a while…

(*The sound of a telephone ringing. Kuan seems dazed.*)

(*Zhong and Da Kou enter at a distance.*)

ZHONG   (*Directly to Kuan.*) Hey, Kuan!

(*Next scene follows closely.*)

第二場：往深圳直通車巴士站／桑拿店

（*香港某往深圳直通車巴士站。*）

大： （*從遠處大叫*）喂！阿寬！

忠： （*從遠處大叫*）呢邊呀！

（*寬清醒過來走到二人前。*）

寬： ……喂……準新郎哥……sorry……

忠： 點先而家？

大： 都嚟得好快喎，「丙」番鑊先囉咩……

（*二人打寬，三人像小孩的打鬧著。*）

寬： （*寬試圖避開*）OK OK！Sorry！

大： （*繼續打寬，寬繼續避*）……等撚咗半粒鐘……

忠： （*繼續打寬，寬繼續避*）……「踏」九嗰班都開埋喇……我有幾「可」出倒嚟吖，「ngei」咗Kitty好耐架。

寬： Sorry囉！（*寬最後逃脱了。*）唔玩呀嘩……

大／忠： 今晚仲唔係你嘅……

（*燈轉。一個空姐服裝的女子出現，她是琪，對著手機。*）

SCENE 2 – BUS STATION TO SHENZHEN/SAUNA SHOP

(*A bus station with services from Hong Kong to Shenzhen.*)

DA (*Loudly from a distance.*) Hey! Kuan!

ZHONG (*Loudly from a distance.*) Over here.

(*Kuan recovers and goes to them.*)

KUAN Hey…Mr. Groom-to-be… Sorry.

ZHONG Now what?

DA He sure got here quick. Let's slug him one first.

(*The two of them hit Kuan. The three play fight like children.*)

KUAN (*Tries to get away.*) OK, OK. Sorry!

DA (*Continues to hit Kuan. Kuan continues to avoid him.*) …We've been fucking waiting for half an hour…

ZHONG (*Continues to hit Kuan. Kuan continues to avoid him.*) …We missed the bus at a quarter to… It's so hard for me to come out. I begged Kitty for hours.

KUAN I'm sorry! (*Tries to get away.*) Stop playing…

DA/ZHONG Dinner is on you tonight.

(*Lights change. A woman dressed as a flight attendant enters. She is Qi. She talks into her mobile phone.*)

琪：　　　黎志寬……你去咗邊，我今日放早呀，你想唔
　　　　　想見我呀，覆我呀！

　　　　　（*琪掛了電話離開。*）

　　　　　（*燈轉。巴士上。*）

寬：　　　今晚食乜？

大：　　　食雀。

寬：　　　咩雀？

大：　　　乜雀都有，鳳凰飛龍宴，總之好嘢啦。

寬：　　　咩嚟架！不如巴蜀風吖，水煮牛肉好食喎！

忠：　　　（*突然加入*）唔好食咁耐喎，仲要買碟。

寬：　　　上網「chur」啦！

忠：　　　Kitty閂電腦都仲係成日搵插蘇架。

大：　　　放心唔會食好耐。因為你今晚仲有「婚前特備
　　　　　節目」。

　　　　　（*大向忠展示其手機中的相片。*）

　　　　　（*燈轉。空姐服裝的琪在舞台另一角對著手
　　　　　機。*）

琪：　　　……你有無搞錯呀，仲係留言……去咗玩定扮
　　　　　勤力呀。打返俾我！

　　　　　（*琪掛了電話，離開。*）

　　　　　（*燈轉至桑拿店門外。*）

QI   Li Zhi Kuan… Where are you? I get off early today. Do you want to see me? Call me.

(*Qi hangs up and exits.*)

(*Lights change. In the bus.*)

KUAN   What should we have for dinner tonight?

DA   Birds.

KUAN   What kind?

DA   All kinds. Phoenix feast. The good stuff.

KUAN   What is it? Why don't we go to Bashu Chic? Their broiled beef is good.

ZHONG   (*Interrupts abruptly.*) We have to finish eating early. We have to buy DVDs.

KUAN   Just download it.

ZHONG   Kitty still pulls the cord when she shuts off the computer.

DA   Don't worry. We'll finish early. Because you still have the "pre-marital program".

(*Da shows Zhong some photos on his mobile phone.*)

(*Lights change. Qi, dressed in flight attendant uniform, enters from another side and speaks into her mobile phone.*)

QI   …Are you kidding me? Voice mail… Are you out having fun somewhere or faking work? Call me!

(*Qi hangs up and exits.*)

(*Lights change to sauna shop exterior.*)

寬：　　（普通話）……不用啦吧。我應該未有時間……你順風吧（突然地）算啦吧…再見面我想不太好…（大聲地轉講廣東話）我真係好忙……算啦好唔好呀（很不耐煩）（普通話）再見……可能可以吧……還有……恭喜你……bye bye（即收線，有點呆）。

　　　　（大口氣沖沖出現，接著忠追上。）

忠：　　你話我呀，嗰幾個姐姐話唔識你呀！

大：　　調情呀，你識條毛咩，頂……（對寬）你同佢講……

寬：　　調情呀，你識條毛咩……

　　　　（大口入桑拿店內，寬的電話響。）

寬：　　（接電話）喂……媽……聽朝？……唔得呀要返工……咩……大聲啲聽唔到……同老豆聽朝咩話……好細聲呀……喂……喂……斷咗線！（收線。）

　　　　（忠望著寬不出聲。）

寬：　　斷咗咯，聽朝瞓醒至算！（停。）嚟啦，搵住骨再講啦！

　　　　（二人離開。）

　　　　（燈暗。）

　　　　（舞台黑暗中出現寬的電話錄音。）

KUAN   (*In Putonghua*)… No need. I don't think I'll have time… Have a safe trip. (*Suddenly.*) Forget it… I don't think we should see each other again… (*Speaks loudly in Cantonese.*) …I am very busy… Can we just let it go? (*Impatiently. In Putonghua*) Goodbye… Perhaps… Also… Congratulations… Bye. (*Hangs up immediately. A little dazed.*)

(*Da Kou enters panting, followed by Zhong.*)

ZHONG   You talking to me? The ladies say they don't know you.

DA   Just flirting. You don't know them either. Dammit… (*To Kuan*) You tell him.

KUAN   Just flirting. You don't know them either…

(*Da Kou enters the sauna shop. Kuan's phone rings.*)

KUAN   (*Answers phone.*) Hello? Mom… Tomorrow morning?… I can't. I have to work… What?… I can't hear you… Do what with dad?… You're speaking too softly… Hello?… Hello?… She hung up! (*Hangs up.*)

(*Zhong silently looks at Kuan.*)

KUAN   We got cut off. It can wait until tomorrow. (*Pause.*) Come on. We'll talk after the massage.

(*They exit. Lights change. In darkness, we hear Kuan's voice mail outgoing message.*)

寬： 　（*VO*）邊位搵阿寬，我而家唔方便聽你嘅電話，我有緊要事做緊，請你留低口訊，我好快會覆返你。（*女聲：請喺「咇」一聲之後留低你嘅口訊*）

　（*此時桑拿浴房同時出現，迷霧加上燈光很暗，隱約看見一男子，他是大口，只圍著毛巾在焗桑拿，靜若石頭一樣，頭頂上一塊小方巾。*）

　（*劇場另一角燈漸亮，出現一女子，她是寬的姐姐，拿著電話。*）

姐： 　（*不滿地*）阿寬，問你啲嘢呀！打返俾我吖。

　（*姐掛了電話，離開。*）

　（*劇場另一角，琪出現拿著電話。*）

寬： 　（*VO*）邊位搵阿寬，我而家唔方便聽你嘅電話，我有緊要事做緊，請你留低口訊，我好快會覆返你。（*女聲：請係「咇」一聲之後留低你嘅口訊。*）

琪： 　已經「咇」咗一聲喇，我而家留言。去咗邊度玩呀？唔理人！打返俾我吖。

KUAN   (*VO*) Who's calling? I can't answer your call right now. I am doing something important now. Please leave a message and I'll get back to you as soon as possible. (*Female voice: "Please leave a message after the beep".*)

(*The sauna room appears in mist and low light. It is dark. We vaguely see a man. It is Da Kou. He is wearing just a towel in the sauna. He sits quietly like a rock. He has a small towel on his head.*)

(*The lights on the other side of the stage change. A woman appears. She is Kuan's sister. She has a phone.*)

SISTER   (*Unhappy*) Kuan. I want to ask you something. Call me back.

(*Sister hangs up and exits.*)

(*On the other side of the stage, Qi appears with a phone.*)

KUAN   (*VO*) Who's calling? I can't answer your call right now. I am doing something important now. Please leave a message and I'll get back to you as soon as possible. (*Female voice: "Please leave a message after the beep".*)

QI   I heard the beep so I'm leaving you a message. Where are you? You didn't call me back. Call me.

（琪掛了電話，離開。）

（此時寬和忠慢慢步入桑拿房，寬坐下，忠坐到大口身邊，大口即起身坐到寬身邊。他們都是把小毛巾放在頭上。三人一起桑拿浴。他們都靜如石頭一樣，但有很深的呼吸聲。不時發出熱力迫人呼氣聲。）

（很長的靜默。）

忠： ……（熱得很舒服地）嘎……（短靜）

寬： （望一眼忠又望一眼大口）……唉……（短靜）

大： （用毛巾抹一抹汗，深深的呼一口氣）……噓……（短靜）

寬： …係咪呢……

大： ……哎……你……老……味……噓……

忠： （很舒服地）……嘩……依也……掂呀……

大： （短靜）（向忠）……掂！？……

寬： ……哈……（短靜）唉……叫……咗……你……架……啦……嘥晒啲時間……

（忠拿起水殼加了一殼水在石頭上，蒸氣的響聲。）

忠： ……嘎……

大： ……嘩……頂……你……吖……

寬： ……頂……

忠： ……頂……我？……我……頂你……

(*Qi hangs up and exits. At this time, Kuan and Zhong stroll into the sauna room. Kuan sits down. Zhong sits next to Da Kou. Da Kou gets up and moves next to Kuan. They both place a small towel over their heads. Three of them are inside the sauna. They are all quiet, sitting like rocks, but breathing deeply, occasionally letting out sighs that indicate the temperature of the room. A long silence.*)

ZHONG   … (*Enjoying the heat*) Ahhh… (*Short silence.*)

KUAN   (*Looks at Zhong and then at Da Kou.*)… Ahhh… (*Short silence.*)

DA   (*Wipes the sweat with his towel. Breathes deeply.*)… Shhh… (*Short silence.*)

KUAN   … I told you…

DA   … Ahhh… Bloody hell… Shhh…

ZHONG   (*With much comfort*) Wow… Ow… So?

DA   (*Short silence. To Zhong*) So?

KUAN   … Ha… (*Short silence.*) Ahh… I… told… you… What a waste of time.

(*Zhong picks up the ladle and scoops water onto the rocks. Steam hisses.*)

ZHONG   … Ahhh…

DA   … Wow… Damn… you…

KUAN   … Damn…

ZHONG   … Damn… me? I… damn you…

寬/大：　　（互望）……屌你……（把小毛巾用力摘向忠）

忠：　　……呀……

（寬、大口起身離開。忠也離開。）

（寬姐再出現某一角，「呎」一聲之後。）

姐：　　你究竟聽唔聽電話呀……聽日得唔閒陪老豆去睇醫生，佢做心電圖，阿媽想你幫手去聽下醫生講乜，我要返工唔去得呀。打返俾我。

（姐掛了電話離開。）

（燈慢慢暗下去同時寬的電話錄音再次出現。）

寬：　　（VO）邊位搵阿寬，我而家唔方便聽你嘅電話，我有緊要事做緊，請你留低口訊，我好快會覆返你。（女聲：請係「呎」一聲之後留低你嘅口訊。）

（很長的「呎」聲。）

（燈轉至按摩房的寬、大口和忠。）

大：　　睇小幾隻碟駛死呀，試嚟試去，等撚咗成粒鐘，返嚟仲話無。我頂你吖。

忠：　　都話Kitty 要揸住集碟至……

KUAN/DA   (*Looking at each other*) ... Fuck you... (*They take their small towels and flick towards Zhong.*)

ZHONG   ...Ow...

(*Kuan and Da Kou get up to leave. Zhong leaves also.*)

(*Kuan's sister enters on another side. Speaks after a "beep".*)

SISTER   Can you not hear your phone? Are you free to take dad to the doctor tomorrow? He needs an ECG. Mom wants you to go and listen to what the doctor says. I can't go. I have to work. Call me.

(*Sister hangs up and exits.*)

(*Light slowly fades. At the same time, Kuan's voice mail is heard.*)

KUAN   (*VO*) Who's calling? I can't answer your call right now. I am doing something important now. Please leave a message and I'll get back to you as soon as possible. (*Female voice: "Please leave a message after the beep".*)

(*Long "beep".*)

(*Lights change to the massage room with Kuan, Da Kou and Zhong.*)

DA   Seeing one less DVD isn't going to kill you.

ZHONG   I told you Kitty won't rest until she has the DVD in her hands.

大： 我揸爆你就真，為女死為女亡。（*説完又把頭轉回朝下。*）

忠： （*突然用雙手撐起上身對大口*）好啦吓！

大： （*仍然面朝下*）……明益你，你條粉腸搞禍晒！

忠： 唔該晒喎！（*説完把頭轉回朝下。*）

大： ……我話你聽（*突然用雙手撐起上身對忠*）啲港女真係無得比！你問下阿寬佢就最清楚嘞！（*説完把頭轉回朝下。*）

寬： （*突然用雙手撐起上身對大口*）講乜嘢呀大口你……

大： （*面仍朝下*）……你嗰個青島姑娘呀……

寬： （*笑著對大口*）癲線咩你……

忠： （*突然用雙手撐起上身對寬*）有啲嘢……

（*寬睡下。*）

大： 無嘢……

忠： 即係有嘢囉，寬，你有個青島姑娘……

大： （*把忠撳低*）八婆。咩嘢都有你份！？（*對寬*）不過你唔要就真嘅晒……

DA	I'm going to kill you with my bare hands. That woman will be the end of you. (*Lowers his head after he speaks.*)
ZHONG	(*Suddenly with arms at waist, raises his chest towards Da Kou.*) That's enough!
DA	(*With head lowered.*) It's for your own good. You've ruined it, you asshole!
ZHONG	Thanks a lot. (*Lowers his head after he speaks.*)
DA	Let me tell ya… (*Suddenly with arms at his waist, raises his chest towards Zhong.*) Hong Kong girls can't compare. Ask Kuan. He knows all about it. (*Lowers his head after he speaks.*)
KUAN	(*Suddenly with arms at his waist, raises his chest towards Da Kou.*) What the hell are you saying, Da Kou?
DA	(*With his head lowered.*) Your Qingdao lady…
KUAN	(*Laughs at Da Kou.*) You're crazy…
ZHONG	(*Suddenly with arms at his waist, raises his chest towards Kuan.*) Something is going on…
	(*Kuan dozes off.*)
DA	Nothing…
ZHONG	That means there's something. Kuan, you have a Qingdao lady…
DA	(*Clenches Zhong.*) You busybody. It's none of your business. (*To Kuan*) But it sure is a waste…

寬： （對大口）喂⋯⋯係咪玩嘢呀而家⋯⋯唔好再講吓。

（寬突然起身離去，忠起身看著寬，大口繼續講不知寬已走。）

大： 我哋祖國地大物博，吓，真係要幾索有幾索佢話你幾「chok」你就有幾「chok」，最重要係⋯⋯佢會俾你知到你係一個男人，佢係一個女人⋯⋯

忠： 你究竟講咩啫！

（燈光轉變同時寬的電話錄音再次出現。）

寬： （VO）邊位搵阿寬，我而家唔方便聽你嘅電話，我有緊要事做緊，請你留低口訊，我好快會覆返你。（女聲：請係「呯」一聲之後留低你嘅口訊。）

（很長的「呯」聲。）

（此場完。）

KUAN (*To Da Kou*) Hey… That's not funny… Stop it.

   (*Suddenly, Kuan gets up and leaves. Zhong gets up and watches Kuan. Da Kou continues, not realizing Kuan has left.*)

DA Our motherland is rich in history and culture. You can get the prettiest girls. The most important thing is… she lets you know that you're a man and she's a woman…

ZHONG What are you talking about?

   (*Lights change. At the same time, Kuan's voice mail sounds again.*)

KUAN (*VO*) Who's calling? I can't answer your call right now. I am doing something important now. Please leave a message and I'll get back to you as soon as possible. (*Female voice: "Please leave a message after the beep".*)

   (*A long beep.*)

   (*End of scene.*)

第三場：琪的家

(*寬剛進門，琪就從房出來身穿空姐制服。*)

琪： Welcome on board, Sir. May I take a look your boarding pass？（*熱情地*）Your seat is right here...

(*琪推了寬坐在沙發，寬莫名其妙地被琪控制著。*)

琪： Ladies and gentlemen, the Captain has turned on the fasten seat belt sign. Please take your seats and fasten your seat belts.

寬： OK OK OK，今日玩呢家嘢！（*普通話*）服務員，先給我來一杯Black Label，再來一份牛排……（*起身*）

琪： （*即接*）咪嘈……（*再推回坐位，拿起咕臣*）Blanket, sir？

寬： 成三十度，唔駛啦掛……

琪： （*用咕臣打寬，即接*）咪嘈。

寬： OK，（*寬起身，普通話*）喂，我跟你說……

琪： 咪嘈啦。（*不好的普通話*）坐下來，閉嘴。

(*寬坐下。*)

(*琪用溫柔令人開心的聲音模擬機艙上的廣播。*)

SCENE 3 – QI'S HOME

(*Kuan has just entered. Qi comes out of her room wearing a flight attendant uniform.*)

QI   Welcome on board, sir. May I take a look at your boarding pass? (*Passionately*) Your seat is right here…

          (*Qi pushes Kuan onto the sofa. Kuan lets himself be controlled by Qi.*)

QI   Ladies and gentlemen, the captain has turned on the fasten seat belt sign. Please take your seats and fasten your seat belts.

KUAN   I see. That's today's game. (*In Putonghua*) Miss flight attendant, one Black Label and then a steak… (*Gets up.*)

QI   (*Follows closely.*) Quiet… (*Pushes him back into the seat. Picks up a cushion.*) Blanket, sir?

KUAN   I don't think so. It's 30 degrees.

QI   (*Hits him with the cushion. Follows closely.*) Quiet.

KUAN   OK. (*Gets up. In Putonghua*) Hey, let me tell you…

QI   Quiet. (*In poor Putonghua*) Sit down. Shut up.

          (*Kuan sits.*)

          (*Qi speaks in a soft and plesant voice, imitating a cabin broadcast.*)

琪： Ladies and gentlemen, my name is Karina and I'm your chief flight attendant. On behalf of Captain BalaBalaBala and the entire crew, welcome aboard Kowloon Airlines flight KO lalala, non-stop service from Hong Kong to Vancouver …

寬： Hong Kong to溫哥華？咪有排坐？（*寬又站起身*）

琪： 咪嘈呀……Ladies and gentlemen呀，你扣咗安全帶啦喇，唔準郁。

（*寬又坐下，把袋中的手提電話拿出。*）

琪： At this time,（*琪把寬的電話搶過來*）we request that all mobile phones and pagers be turned off. And we also request your full attention…

寬： （*舉手發問*）小姐。我有急切需要。

琪： （*把寬推回沙發*）During a decompression, an oxygen mask will automatically appear in front of you. To start the flow of oxygen, pull the mask towards you. Place it firmly over your nose and mouth.（*用雙手「meet」寬的面。*）

寬： 我需要人工呼吸同制服誘惑。（*一手把琪拉到坐在自己身上。*）

琪： Ladies and gentlemen呀，（*兩人扭作一團又笑又打，琪欲掙扎逃離寬。*）喂呀你fasten咗seat belt架喇，坐返埋位啦。喂呀，喂呀turbulence。

QI	Ladies and gentlemen, my name is Karina and I'm your chief flight attendant. On behalf of Captain Blahblahblah and the entire crew, welcome aboard Kowloon Airlines Flight KO lalala, non-stop service from Hong Kong to Vancouver…
KUAN	Hong Kong to Vancouver? That's a long flight! (*Stands up again.*)
QI	Quiet! Ladies and gentlemen, you have already fastened your seat belts. Don't move.
	(*Kuan sits down again. Takes out his mobile phone.*)
QI	At this time, we request that all mobile phones and pagers be turned off. (*Qi takes away Kuan's mobile phone.*) And we also request your full attention…
KUAN	(*Raises his hand to ask*) Miss, I have urgent needs.
QI	(*Pushes Kuan onto the sofa.*) During a decompression, an oxygen mask will automatically appear in front of you. To start the flow of oxygen, pull the mask towards you. Place it firmly over your nose and mouth. (*Uses her hands to pinch Kuan's face.*)
KUAN	I need mouth-to-mouth resuscitation from someone in a seductive uniform. (*Pulls Qi towards him.*)
QI	Hey, ladies and gentlemen! (*They tussle with laughter. Qi tries to escape from Kuan.*) You have already fastened your seat belts. Sit down. Hey… Hey….

寬：　係呀，very危險呀，你快啲攬著我啦……

琪：　（不滿）Ladies and gentlemen呀，Please return to your seats and keep your seat belts fastened呀。Thank you. 唔玩呀……

寬：　係你玩先喎……擺明制服誘惑我啦……

琪：　……整「巢」晒套衫……

琪：　（掙扎逃脫，不滿地）yea……（琪打寬）搞住晒，唔玩嘞！

寬：　你咁嘅服務要賠償，肉償啦……除衫……

琪：　痴線，我服務一流呀，坐番低啦，唔玩……

寬：　唔玩？……唔賠錢就賠瞓……（再出手）

琪：　仲嚟……唔玩啦……Stop……引擎出煙……

　　　（兩人互相追逐。）

寬：　話知佢，出嘢就真……

琪：　Stop!（把寬推倒在沙發。）

　　　（最後琪逃離了寬。）

寬：　點先，而家旅程唔愉快喎。

琪：　你自己攞嚟嘅。叫機場特警拉你添呀！

寬：　唔玩喇？

琪：　唔玩。「巢」晒啦套衫。

KUAN   Oh yes, very dangerous. You better hold onto me...

QI   (*Unhappily*) Hey, ladies and gentlemen. Please return to your seats and keep your seat belts fastened. Thank you. Stop it...

KUAN   You started it... Obviously you want to seduce me with your uniform.

QI   You're wrinkling it...

QI   (*Tries to escape. Unhappily*) Hey... (*Hits Kuan.*) You've messed it up. Stop it.

KUAN   You have to compensate for such poor service. Compensation of the flesh... Take it off...

QI   You're crazy. My service is the best. Sit down. I'm not playing anymore...

KUAN   You're not playing? Then you'll have to compensate in the bedroom... (*Tries again.*)

QI   Stop it!... Stop! Engine trouble...

         (*They chase each other.*)

KUAN   So what. I don't care...

QI   STOP! (*Pushes Kuan onto the sofa.*)

         (*Finally, Qi escapes from Kuan.*)

KUAN   Now what? I didn't enjoy my journey.

QI   It's your own fault. I'll get the airport police to arrest you.

KUAN   No more?

QI   No. My uniform is all wrinkled.

寬：　OK，尿尿。（*起身入了廁所，剩下琪一人。*）今日就係學呢啲呀？你嘅普通話進步咗喎，「閉嘴」都識講！

琪：　（*一邊整理制服一邊對廁所的寬*）我不「嬲」都唔差架。喺嗰班衰嘢成日笑我之嘛，我一開聲佢哋就「暗」住半邊嘴。我根本就無問題，（*普通話*）我……沒……問題……的！（*對廁所內大聲地*）你話係咪？

寬：　（*在廁所內*）沒……「有」問題！

琪：　第時我實淨係飛美加，English only囉。

寬：　咁就真係「沒問題」，不過一去就五六日喎。

琪：　仲好可以成日返屋企；唔駛媽咪成日哦我。

寬：　（*在廁所內*）咁我點呀？

琪：　你諗你喇，我「玩」下手唔返架喇，daddy mummy養，唔駛做添呀。

寬：　（*在廁所內*）唔怕悶咪唔好返囉，我去搵二奶。

（*琪突然停了下來望著廁所。*）

琪：　尋晚打幾次俾你，你都唔聽。

寬：　（*在廁所內*）擺咗locker度吖嗎，揼骨點聽啫！

KUAN   OK. Wee wee. (*Gets up to go to the bathroom, leaving Qi by herself.*) That's what you learned today? Your Putonghua is improving. You can say "shut up".

QI   (*Fixes her uniform and approaches Kuan in the bathroom.*) It's not that bad to begin with. They just keep laughing at me. Every time I open my mouth, they can't contain their laughter. I don't have a problem with it. (*In Putonghua*) I... have no problem! (*Loudly towards the bathroom*) Don't you agree?

KUAN   (*From the bathroom*) No problem... Not!

QI   Then I'll just fly North American routes. English only.

KUAN   Then there won't be any more problems. But you'll be gone for five or six days at a time.

QI   And it will be like going home. My mom can stop whining.

KUAN   (*From the bathroom*) What about me?

QI   You better figure it out yourself. Maybe I won't come back. My mom and dad can take care of me. I don't have to work.

KUAN   (*From the bathroom*) If you can handle the boredom, don't come back. I'll get a mistress.

    (*Qi suddenly stops and looks at the bathroom.*)

QI   I called you a few times last night. You didn't answer.

KUAN   (*From the bathroom*) I was at my massage. The phone was in the locker.

琪： 之後又唔覆？問你今晚屋企食定出街食呀。

寬： （*在廁所內*）得啦⋯⋯又唔係有啲乜⋯⋯咁緊張做乜⋯⋯

琪： 咁要個電話嚟做乜啫？

（*寬的電話響。*）

琪： 嗱，無用嘅電話又響喇。（*琪凝看電話顯示然後停了下來。*）喂呀，無來電呀，聽唔聽呀？

寬： （*在廁所內*）幫我聽，叫佢等陣。

琪： （*急接電話*）喂⋯⋯（*電話收線了。*）
喂⋯⋯喂。

（*寬回來。*）

寬： 咩⋯⋯

琪： 收咗線，無出聲。

寬： （*接過電話*）哦⋯⋯由佢囉。

（*琪看住寬，停。*）

琪： （*輕鬆地*）咩呀，尋晚無俾二奶家用呀？

寬： 咁都俾你估倒⋯⋯

琪： 好似係女人嚟喎⋯⋯

寬： 呢個世界唔係女人就男人架啦⋯⋯

琪： 即係係啦⋯⋯

QI	Then why didn't you call me back? I wanted to ask if you wanted to eat out tonight or stay home.
KUAN	(*From the bathroom*) Yeah... No big deal... What's the rush?
QI	Then what good is the phone?

(*Kuan's phone rings.*)

QI	See? Your useless phone is ringing again. (*Qi stares at the phone display and then stops.*) Hey, there's no caller display. You want to answer it?
KUAN	(*From the bathroom*) Answer it for me. Tell him to wait.
QI	(*Rushes to answer phone.*) Hello?... (*The line is dead.*) Hello? Hello?

(*Kuan returns.*)

KUAN	What?
QI	Hung up. Didn't say anything.
KUAN	(*Takes the phone.*) Oh... whatever.

(*Qi watches Kuan. Stops.*)

QI	(*Lightly*) So? You didn't give money to your mistress last night?
KUAN	How did you know?
QI	I think it was a woman...
KUAN	If it wasn't a man, it was a woman...
QI	So it was a woman...

寬：	又話無出聲……
琪：	係呀……
寬：	又點知係女人呀？
琪：	佢「吖」咗一吓……
寬：	「吖」「吖」「吖」……
琪：	我聽倒佢唞氣……
寬：	「霞」「霞」「霞」……廠打嚟掛！
	（寬看電話。）
寬：	食日本嘢吖，我請！？
琪：	做乜轉話題呀？
寬：	咩轉話題……
琪：	無咩？
寬：	咩呀……你問我食咩呀嗎？
琪：	咁無囉……
	（一頓。）
寬：	咁今晚食咩呀……
琪：	（即接）唔想出去喇！
寬：	咁自己煮囉……
琪：	（即接）你尋晚又唔聽電話，我乜都無買。
寬：	出去食囉。
琪：	（即接）都話唔出咯，聽朝早堂呀，食公仔麵囉。
	（一頓。）

KUAN   You said she didn't say anything…

QI   Yeah…

KUAN   Then how do you know it was a woman?

QI   She "ahhh-ed".

KUAN   Ah… Ah… Ah…

QI   I heard her breathe…

KUAN   "Ha… ha… ha…" … Maybe it was the factory.

        (*Kuan looks at the phone.*)

KUAN   Let's have Japanese food. My treat.

QI   Why are you changing the subject?

KUAN   I didn't.

QI   Didn't you?

KUAN   What… You wanted to ask me what I wanted to eat, right?

QI   Forget it.

        (*A moment.*)

KUAN   So where should we eat?

QI   (*Follows closely.*) I don't want to go out!

KUAN   Then we'll cook…

QI   (*Follows closely.*) You didn't answer your phone last night. I didn't go shopping.

KUAN   Then let's go out.

QI   (*Follows closely.*) I said I don't want to go out. I have an early class tomorrow. Let's have instant noodles.

        (*A moment.*)

寬：　　　（刻意地）喂……我點可以餓親你架……？

琪：　　　（突然按捺住激動）黎志寬，你好嘢。食自己啦你。

寬：　　　我特登嚟陪你食飯喎。

琪：　　　你話食就食我咪好無面。

寬：　　　咁我返屋企同阿媽食架喇。

　　　　　（寬電話又響。）

寬：　　　（看電話再接聽）嗱，真係阿媽。開飯喇。

　　　　　（琪去打寬，寬一面講電話一面對抗攻擊。）

寬：　　　喂，媽，開飯喇，（對琪）你仲嚟（琪騎上了寬的背。）……吓……咩話……（對琪）唔玩住，聽唔到呀。（琪停了聲但還是無聲但大動作的打寬。）（寬對電話）邊間話……我打俾家姐……打咗喇……我而家嚟，你唔好驚，我依家嚟。（寬收線呆了，琪還在背上看寬的無反應。）

琪：　　　咩呀？

寬：　　　老豆突然喺的士度暈咗，依家入咗急症室。

　　　　　（此場完。）

KUAN	(*Purposefully*) Hey... I can't starve you like that...
QI	(*Suddenly with controlled emotion*) Way to go, Li Zhi Kuan. You go ahead and eat.
KUAN	I came to eat with you.
QI	So I'm supposed to eat whenever you please? That's insulting.
KUAN	Then I'll go back to my mother's to eat.
	(*Kuan's phone rings again.*)
KUAN	(*Looks at phone and then answers.*) See, it's mom. Dinner is ready.
	(*Qi attacks Kuan. Kuan answers the phone as he defends himself.*)
KUAN	Hello, Mom? Dinner is ready? (*To Qi*) Stop it. (*Qi jumps onto Kuan's back.*) Huh?... What?... (*To Qi*) Stop playing. I can't hear her. (*Qi stops making noise but continues to hit Kuan in silence. Kuan speaks to phone.*) Which one? I'll call sister... You called her?... I'll call her now... Don't worry, I'll call her now. (*Kuan hangs up and is dazed. Qi is still on Kuan's back. He does not react to her.*)
QI	What is it?
KUAN	My dad suddenly fainted in the taxi. He's at emergency now.
	(*End of scene.*)

第四場：深切治療病房外

（*深夜，長椅上寬坐著，寬的家姐坐著睡了。*）

（*靜默。*）

（*琪從病房出來，然後坐到寬身邊。*）

琪： 喂……

寬： （*望一望琪又回頭靜下來。*）……唔……

琪： 佢隻眼仲有少少斬斬吓，我同佢細細聲講話我走先，佢好似聽到咁架。

寬： ……唔……

（*一頓。*）

琪： 你阿媽仲唔返嘅？

寬： 我去搵佢……（*起身。*）返嚟同你去搭車。

琪： 一齊去吖。

寬： 唔好喇，家姐醒咗得一個人。

姐： （*沒有打開眼沒有任何動作，忽然慢慢地*）同佢搭車啦，走先啦阿琪，夜喇！

寬： 咁同你落去搭車。

（*寬媽入，手上提著便利店膠袋。*）

寬： 媽，去邊呀……咁耐嘅？阿琪走先，佢聽朝開早！

SCENE 4 – OUTSIDE THE INTENSIVE CARE UNIT

(*Late night. Kuan is seated on a long bench. Sister is sleeping on the bench.*)

(*Silence.*)

(*Qi comes out of the intensive care unit and sits next to Kuan.*)

QI   Hey…

KUAN   (*Looks at Qi and is quiet again.*) Mm…

QI   His eyes are still blinking. I whispered in his ear that I was leaving. I think he heard me.

KUAN   Mm…

            (*A moment.*)

QI   How come your mom hasn't returned?

KUAN   I'll go find her… (*Rises.*) When I come back, I'll walk you to a taxi.

QI   I'll go with you.

KUAN   No. When sister wakes up, she'll be alone.

SISTER   (*Without stirring or opening her eyes, suddenly and slowly*) Walk her to a cab. Qi, go home. It's late.

KUAN   I'll walk you to a cab.

            (*Kuan's mother enters with bags from a convenience store.*)

KUAN   Mom, you were gone for so long. Where have you been? Qi has to leave. She has to work early tomorrow.

媽：　　　去埋廁所之嘛。係啦，走先啦，夜啦。買咗啲餅同豆奶，水呀，攞包一路行一路食吖。（*遞給琪。*）

琪：　　　哦，（*接了餅和豆奶*）伯母，你都係返去啦，兜咗你先吖。

媽：　　　唔駛，你哋開工，走先啦。同埋家姐走啦！（*自己拿了餅和一包豆奶，把剩下全袋給寬。*）嗱，一路行一路食啦。

　　　　　（*媽拍拍睡著的姐，姐還是沒有任何動作。*）

姐：　　　（*又慢慢地*）媽你返去啦，瞓醒聽朝再嚟啦，今晚我同阿寬喺度咪得囉。

媽：　　　走啦。我肚餓……（*就坐下開始食不理他們。*）寬，行啦！

寬：　　　（*對琪*）我同你搭車。家姐，你走唔走呀？

　　　　　（*姐用手勢示意他們先走。*）

寬：　　　媽，我同佢落去搭車就返嚟。

琪：　　　伯母，家姐，走先啦，聽日再嚟。

　　　　　（*寬和琪離開剩下兩母女。*）

媽：　　　（*一面食*）叫你返去咯，又話個女要考試。

MOTHER	I just went to the washroom. Oh yes, you go ahead and leave. It's late. I bought some cake, soya milk and water. Take one for the road. (*Hands it to Qi.*)
QI	Oh! (*Takes cake and soya milk.*) Auntie, you should go home too. I can give you a ride.
MOTHER	No. You need to work. You go ahead. Go with Sister. (*She takes out cake and soya milk. Gives the rest to Kuan.*) Here. Eat it on the way home.

(*Mother pats Sister, who was asleep. Sister does not move.*)

SISTER	(*Again, slowly*). Mom, you go home first. Come back tomorrow after a good night's sleep. Kuan and I can stay here tonight.
MOTHER	Go home. I'm hungry... (*Sits down and starts eating, ignoring them.*) Kuan, go!
KUAN	(*To Qi.*) I'll grab a cab with you. Sister, are you leaving?

(*Sister signals for them to leave first.*)

KUAN	Mom, I'll take Qi to a cab first, then I'll come back.
QI	Auntie, Sister, I'm off. See you tomorrow.

(*Kuan and Qi leave Mother and Sister.*)

MOTHER	(*Eating*) I told you to leave. You said your daughter has exams.

姐： 唉（*終於開眼坐起，在膠袋找了樽水，打開就飲了一半。*）打咗電話俾呀頭，聽日唔返早。你走啦，一陣阿寬返嚟叫佢同你返去。

媽： （*快而堅決地*）唔駛，我唔眼瞓。唔走你就瞓啦！（*媽繼續食餅。*）

（*寬回來。*）

姐： 咁快！

寬： 得啦！自己走都得啦，同佢搭咗「leap」咯。

姐： （*凝視著寬*）吓……

（*寬坐下，靜。*）

姐： （*忽然對寬，不太滿意地*）你好忙咩，成日要上去廠呀！同老豆去睇下醫生都唔得。如果早個日做埋個檢查就未必有事。唔駛而家咁，插晒野。

媽： 咪嘈啦，佢要返工咯，你嘈乜啫！

姐： 阿媽邊度識聽啲醫生噏乜鬼野啫。你老豆出得聲就梗係自己都頂唔住至講嘅，佢話得個心口戚住實唔嘢少。

寬： 咪話個心口戚戚下咁羅，都睇咗話心電圖正常咯。不過最好做埋個乜嘢吹氣嗰個就穩陣啲咁囉！

SISTER   (*Sighs. Finally, she opens her eyes. Takes out a bottle of water from the plastic bag and drinks half of it.*) I called my boss. I can take the morning off. You go home. When Kuan comes back, tell him to take you home.

MOTHER   (*Quickly, persisting*) No. I'm not tired. If you won't leave, then sleep. (*Mother continues to eat cake.*)

(*Kuan returns.*)

SISTER   That was fast.

KUAN   I took her to the elevator. She went down by herself. She'll be fine.

SISTER   (*Stares at Kuan.*) What?

(*Kuan sits down. Silence.*)

SISTER   (*Suddenly to Kuan, very annoyed.*) Are you so busy? You have to be at the factory all day? You can't even go to the doctor's with dad? If he'd had those tests earlier this might not have happened. He wouldn't need to be stuck with tubes all over.

MOTHER   Stop it. He has to work. What are you shouting about!

SISTER   Mom doesn't understand what the doctors say. If dad said something then he must have been in real pain. He said he felt tightness in his chest. That couldn't have been a small matter.

KUAN   He just said his chest felt tight The ECG said everything was normal. He could be stabilized with that balloon treatment thing, that's all!

姐： 醫生叫佢最好嗰日即刻去做埋呀，佢又唔識你阿媽又唔識，實話遲啲至睇架，今日唔係佢仲覺戚戚下佢都未必去呀！

寬： 我真係有嘢做呀。

姐： 邊有咁啱架啫，早一日得，遲一日都得，就係嗰日行唔開呀。

寬： 幾個大老細係度開會呀，我點走呀。都費事同你講。

媽： 唏，係度嘈，好睇呀。唔好講。

（*寬起身入了病房。*）

姐： 都唔細架啦，唔怪得搵個咁嘅女朋友，一擔擔，兩個都大唔透。嗰個阿琪又係傻架，搵佢做男朋友，實散架佢地！成日遊戲人間。

媽： 你咪咁勞嘈啦！

姐： 我幫你話佢你話返我，嘩，媽你都得。

（*一頓。*）

姐： 老豆醒唔番我睇佢點。

媽： 唔醒架啦！

（*姐一怔再望一望媽，一頓。*）

SISTER   The doctor said he should have had the treatment that same day. He doesn't understand and neither does mom. Of course they say they'll take care of it later. If he hadn't felt tightness today, he may not have come at all!

KUAN   I was busy.

SISTER   What a coincidence. You had to be busy on the exact day of the appointment.

KUAN   My bosses were having a meeting. I couldn't leave. Forget it.

MOTHER   Hey, stop it. You're making a scene.

(*Kuan gets up and goes into the ICU room.*)

SISTER   He's not young anymore. No wonder he chose that kind of girlfriend. They're both kids. Qi is so stupid, going out with him. Everything is just a game to them. They're doomed.

MOTHER   Stop nagging him!

SISTER   You're blaming me? I'm teaching him for you. Thanks, Mom.

(*A moment.*)

SISTER   I wonder what he'll do if dad doesn't wake up.

MOTHER   He will never wake up!

(*Sister looks at Mother in silence. A moment.*)

媽： 以前工友個老公咪係咁，喺廳梳化度瞓覺，到我工友煮完飯出去叫醒佢食飯至知原來都無氣咯。就咁瞓瞓下就咁去咗自己都唔知。都好⋯⋯唔駛捱。好過嗰啲痛餐死又死唔去嗰啲。

姐： 講咩啫媽你⋯⋯

媽： 好彩今日我話搭的士，佢仲話坐巴士去得咯喎。唔係而家，連喉都唔駛插！

（*靜。*）

（*寬急步走出來。*）

寬： 媽，快啲入去！

（*姐即入，媽停了一下，把最後一口豆奶喝完，將豆奶盒放回便利店膠袋起身入內。*）

（*燈即轉，剩下寬在舞台。*）

寬： 有一晚我好夜至返屋企，幾晚無返架喇。我一開門，燈已經熄咗，我以為無人。間屋好靜，好似好耐無返過嚟咁。行過老竇房，我見到佢已經瞓咗覺，得佢一個。我就想返房。行過嗰陣我望咗一望老竇瞓覺個樣，佢瞓得好靜，郁都唔郁，口有小小打開。我好耐無咁樣望住我老竇。佢唔同咗，同我印象嘅老竇有啲唔同。肥咗，兩邊面同下巴啲皮「dum」咗。鼻毛長到凸咗出嚟。啲皮膚好粗多咗皺紋。原來佢

MOTHER   The same thing happened to my co-worker's husband. He fell asleep on the sofa. When my colleague finished dinner, she went to call him and realized he had stopped breathing. That's how he went, without even knowing it. That's good though... No pain. It's better than suffering a lot and still you don't die.

SISTER   What are you talking about, mom?

MOTHER   Good thing I said to take a cab today. He wanted to take a bus. If we had, he may not have needed the tubes at all!

(*Silence.*)

(*Kuan rushes from inside.*)

KUAN   Mom, hurry. Come in!

(*Sister rushes in. Mother stops. Drinks the last sip of soya milk. Places the milk box into the convenience store plastic bag.*)

(*Lights change. Kuan is the only one left on stage.*)

KUAN   One night, I got home very late. I hadn't been home for a few nights in a row. When I opened the door, the lights were already off. I thought no one was there. The house was quiet. I felt like I hadn't been there for a long time. I walked past dad's room. He was already asleep. He was alone. So I was about to go into my room. When I walked past, I looked at my father asleep. He was very quiet. He didn't move. His mouth was

仲有好多白頭髮。佢無打鼻鼾，唔郁，好靜。我個腦閃咗一下。突然我個心寒咗一寒，頭皮開始發麻。我望住佢。佢真係郁都無郁，平時佢會打鼻鼾架，而家無。我將我耳仔「控」埋去佢個鼻度。我同佢塊面好近，我記憶中我大個之後都無試過有同佢咁近。無……咩都無。突然佢嗰口「乎」咗一下。嚇死我。我鬆咗口氣。我行返自己房。我坐咗喺床度同自己講：好彩唔係。（*停*）嗰晚之後我間唔中都會喺返屋企開門嘅時候……個心離一離。

不過呢一日……真係嚟咗。

（*此場完。*）

slightly open. I hadn't looked at my father for a while. He had changed. He seemed different from my impression of him. Fatter. His face and chin were flabbier. His nose hair was sticking out. His skin was rougher and more wrinkled. I realized that his hair was a lot whiter. He wasn't snoring. He was still. Very quiet. My mind flashed. Suddenly my skin grew cold. My scalp was numb. I looked at him. He was completely motionless. Usually, he snored, but right now he wasn't. I put my ear close to his nose. My face was very close to his. I couldn't remember being that close to him since I grew up. Nothing... Nothing at all. Suddenly, he exhaled through his mouth. It scared me. I breathed a sigh of relief. I walked into my room. I sat on my bed and said to myself, "Thank god he wasn't." (*Pause.*) Since that night, every once in a while, I would walk into the house... and my heart would skip a beat. But this day... finally arrived.

(*End of scene.*)

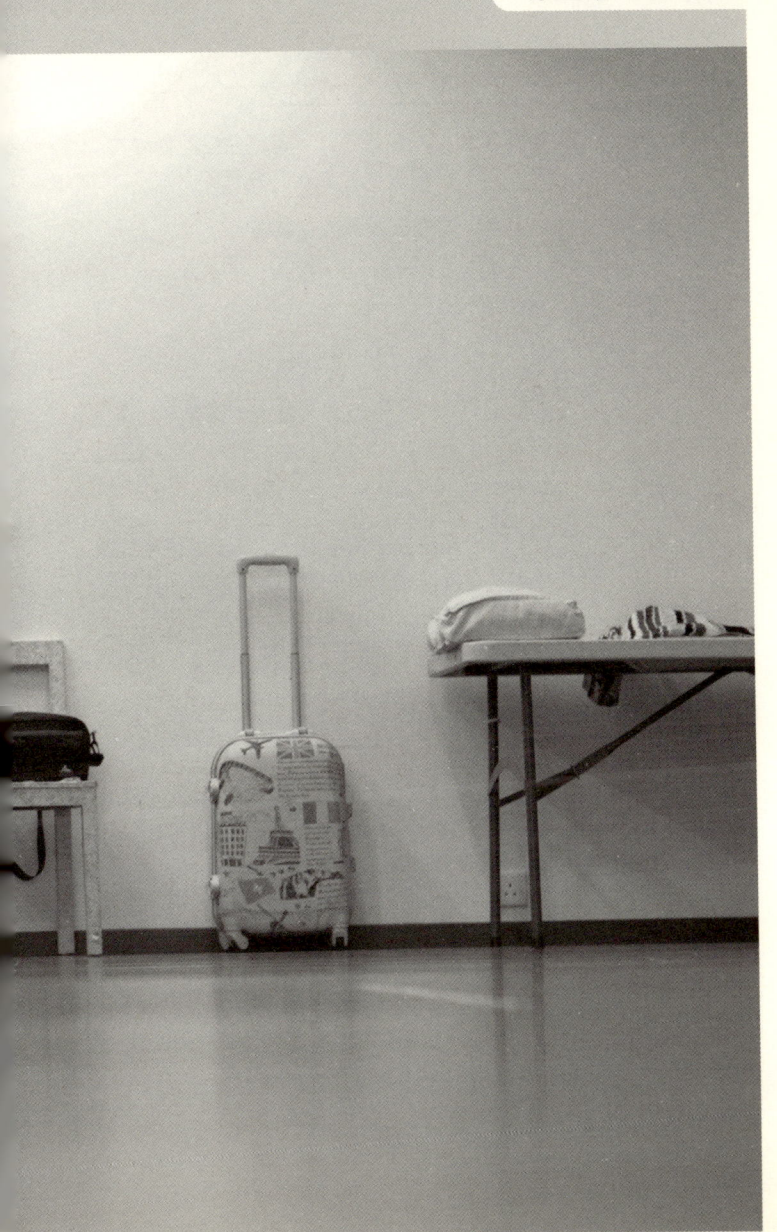

第五場：寬媽的家

（*廳中放了一大堆衣物，寬媽在分配幾堆衣服，再把一些摺好的放入紅白藍袋。*）

媽： （*向內*）幫我去攞幾個膠袋嚟。

（*寬帶著膠袋出，手上拿著一本銀行簿和一個銀包。*）

寬： 嗱（*把膠袋給寬媽*）……駛乜而家執呀？

媽： 都無用咯，嚟，一份入一袋，一條褲，一件衫。

寬： 做乜？

媽： 打齋嗰日帶埋去俾家姐佢哋，條褲即係老豆留返啲富貴俾你哋，保佑你哋大富大貴。件衫要嚟留念，第時就攞出嚟望下。鍾意邊件你自己揀。第時我死埋你都係咁照做啦。

（*靜。*）

媽： 嗱，入好一人一袋俾家姐。

（*寬照做，寬媽繼續把每件衫看一看，拿起其中幾件。*）

SCENE 5 – KUAN'S MOTHER'S HOME

(*There is much clothing in the living room. Kuan's mother is dividing clothes into different piles. She places some folded ones into a red-white-blue plastic bag.*)

MOTHER (*To offstage*) Bring me a few plastic bags.

(*Kuan enters with bags, as well as a bankbook and a wallet.*)

KUAN Here. (*Gives bags to Mother.*)… You don't need to pack now, do you?

MOTHER They're useless. Here, a bag for each of you. One pair of pants and one shirt.

KUAN What for?

MOTHER Take it to your sister at the Tao prayer ceremony. The pants signify the wealth that your father has left you, for the prosperity blessing. The shirt is a souvenir. You can look at it every once in a while. Take whichever one you like. When I die, you do the same for me.

(*Silence.*)

MOTHER Here. Finish packing a bag for your sister.

(*Kuan does as he is told. Mother continues to look through clothing. She picks up a few pieces.*)

媽： 買俾佢都唔著，呢幾件永安買架，四百幾蚊件架，成日就係著埋嗰件爛鬼梅菜，嗰條領都黃晒佢都仲著，真係核鬼突。（*把剩下的衣物放入紅白藍膠袋。*）呢啲嗰日攞埋去燒埋佢。

寬： 仲有裡面櫃啲襪呢，都燒呀。

媽： 佢鍾意嗰兩件今朝都著咗咯。攞去樓下啲箱捐埋俾人囉！

寬： 咪依家執啦，瞓啦，搞咗一日，今朝又咁早起身！

（*媽繼續執衫。*）

寬： 搵日同你去金鐘嗰度搞埋佢銀行啲錢。

媽： 你攞埋佢啦，仲要駛嗰啲錢咪用埋佢囉。

寬： 嗰啲我會同家姐搞架啦。唔駛用佢嘅。呢度得幾千蚊，你攞返啦。

媽： 唔叫佢去攞生果金佢都唔會開本簿仔。

寬： 睇吓邊日我同你去。唔通益埋銀行呀！

媽： 佢成世人一出糧就俾晒我，淨係攞夠食。係食煙衰，唔食咪好囉！

（*媽突然停了，把地上幾包煙遞給寬。*）

MOTHER	He never wore what you bought him. We bought these at Wing On. Four hundred dollars each! But he wore the same ragged old clothes, even when there were rings around the collar. So gross. (*Puts the remainder of the clothing into the red-white-blue bags.*) Take these to burn that day.
KUAN	What about the coats in the closet? You want to burn those too?
MOTHER	He's already wearing the two that he liked. Take the rest to the charity box.
KUAN	Pack up later. You should rest. It's been a long day. You woke up so early.

(*Mother continues to pack clothing.*)

KUAN	We should go to Admiralty one of these days to withdraw the rest of his money.
MOTHER	You take it. Spend it on whatever you need.
KUAN	I'll figure all that out with Sister. We don't need the money. I have a few thousand here. Take it.
MOTHER	If I had never told him to collect his "fruit money", he'd never have opened an account.
KUAN	We'll go one day. We shouldn't let the bank have it.
MOTHER	All his life, he gave me every cent he made. He only took food money. Cigarettes were his only vice. He should have quit smoking!

(*Mother stops suddenly. Picks up a few packs of cigarettes off the floor for Kuan.*)

媽： 　　　佢「劑」喺櫃筒架。打齋嗰日攞埋去俾佢啦。

（*媽終於停下來坐著。*）

（*靜。*）

媽： 　　　真係點諗倒佢會無端端就去……（*停。*）唉，隻眼好赤，我瞓。

寬： 　　　瞓啦，啲衫由佢，聽日至執。

媽： 　　　你都早啲瞓。（*媽入房。*）

（*剩下寬，寬把地上幾袋的衫搬上沙發，在當中拿起一件淺綠色的衫，看得出是很久沒有穿過的衣服，突然凝住了，看著它。*）

（*此場完。*）

MOTHER   He kept them in the drawer. Bring them to him on the day of the ceremony.

          (*Mother finally stops and sits down.*)

          (*Silence.*)

MOTHER   Who could have guessed he would go so suddenly… (*Pause. She sighs.*) My eyes are sore. I'm going to sleep.

KUAN   You go to bed. Leave the clothes. Pack tomorrow.

MOTHER   Don't stay up too late. (*Mother goes into bedroom.*)

          (*Kuan is alone. He picks up the piles of clothes from the floor and places them on the sofa. He picks out a pale green shirt and realizes that it hasn't been worn for a long time. Kuan stops and looks at it.*)

          (*End of scene.*)

第六場：某酒吧一角

（*寬沉默地在不停飲酒，忠有些勞氣。*）

忠： 啲相呀⋯⋯咁呀⋯⋯總之乜鬼嘢我尋晚都一次過擺晒出嚟擺晒係老婆面前，同佢講邊樣係幾時送嘅，邊樣又係幾時嘅，逐件逐件同佢講。諗住講完就無事啦。唉！唔講猶自可，講咗仲仆街，佢話「咁即係你仲好記得佢啦，乜都記得咁清楚」。喂，大佬呀，又係你叫我講，講唔出就掉咗佢架。咁我講出嚟你又發我爛渣。咁算點呀。

寬： 你又係嘅，同何倚雯啲嘢你仲留住佢。

忠： 喂！初戀一世人得一次咋。一世人一次嗰啲嘢點都要記住架吓話。我淨係想間唔中懷緬吓啫。

寬： 即係好似拜山咁。

忠： 我講到第二張相咋，就發晒癲咁。「咁做乜仲同我結婚？仲有無同嗰隻狐狸精見面」，佢都癡線。狐狸精！十幾廿年前啦。

寬： 你做乜真係信佢⋯⋯講佢知啫。佢會唔會講以前啲嘢你聽吖？

忠： 唉！佢地唔計架。你想同佢用番同一招呀！你都唔駛旨意⋯⋯

寬： 所以⋯ ⋯結婚嚟做乜呢？

SCENE 6 – THE CORNER OF SOME BAR

(Kuan is drinking quietly and continuously. Zhong seems slightly peeved.)

ZHONG   Photos… cards… I took out everything I had to show my wife last night, to tell her who gave it to me and when. I told her about every item. I thought if I told her everything, I'd be fine. Oh boy… I should have said nothing, because now I am fucked. She said, "That means you remember every one of them very clearly." Come on, man, you told me to tell you! You said if I didn't tell you, I'd have to throw it away. Now that I've told you, you blow up on me. What the hell is that?

KUAN   You're an idiot. You shouldn't have kept the things He Yi Wen gave you.

ZHONG   Hey. You only have one first love. You always remember that stuff. I just want to think about it once in a while.

KUAN   Like paying respects to your dearly departed.

ZHONG   She started going crazy on the second photo. "Then why did you marry me? Have you been seeing that bitch"? She's crazy. "That bitch"! I haven't seen her in almost 20 years.

KUAN   Why did you believe her? Just tell her?! Would she tell you about her exes?

ZHONG   *(Sighs.)* That's not how they think about it. You want to use the same strategy? Forget it.

KUAN   So… why get married?

忠： 老婆我娶咗，我好「老黎」佢，到我死我都會記住同佢結婚嗰日。咁初戀，我戀過架嗎，點會唔記得啫！

寬： 咁你記唔記得你隻豬俾咗邊個呀又？

忠： 緊記得，不知幾蕩氣迴腸。

寬： 即係唔係何倚雯囉！

忠： 我嗰陣準備好俾佢架喎。OK吖佢……嗰陣！你嗰陣返團契都係因為佢啫吓話。

寬： 我定你呀。

忠： 嘩，尋晚仲有一張相係我哋三個一齊影架。考完「Cert」團契去屯門宿營嗰次呀！

寬： 係你要同人影相又驚拉埋我咋。你拉我埋去嗰陣……佢仲白咗我一眼。

忠： 你開咗個頭又唔理佢。搞到人哋……無疾而終……

寬： 我搞佢！我幾時搞過佢呀！係都係佢自己攞㗎。早知去獨木舟露營好過！嗰晚真係恐怖呀。好似去咗邪教咁。

忠： 咁你去得團契都預咗要架啦。

ZHONG	I married my wife. I love her. I'll remember our wedding anniversary until the day I die. But your first love… My first love… How could I forget it?!
KUAN	Do you remember who ate your cherry?
ZHONG	Of course! It was unforgettable.
KUAN	So it wasn't He Yi Wen.
ZHONG	But I would have given it to her. She was OK too… then! You used to go to the fellowship because of her, right?
KUAN	You or me?
ZHONG	I found a photo last night of the three of us. That time when we all went to camp at Tuen Mun after the cert exam.
KUAN	You're the one who wanted a photo with her, but you dragged me along. You dragged me along, and that's when she noticed me.
ZHONG	You started something with her and never followed through. I had to… carry through, naturally.
KUAN	I started something? When did I start something? If there was anything, she started it. We should have gone to the canoeing camp instead. That night was scary. It was like a cult.
ZHONG	When you joined the fellowship, you knew it would be like that.

寬： 幾十人困埋喺一齊，熄晒燈輪流喺度向神決志，決完就揸住支蠟燭喺度滴蠟，喊到阿媽都唔認得。呀何倚雯佢呀……真係Oh my god，足足講咗「三個字」咁耐，好似鬼上身咁，喊到豬頭咁呀佢，嘩！索下索下喺度「神呀，我將自己交託喺你手上」……真係oh my god呀。嗰十五分鐘之後我就肯定我同阿God唔會friend架，我同佢就更加唔可以friend添。

忠： 你唔信咪唔信囉，人哋有宗教自由嘅。

寬： 如果你仲同佢一齊……睇吓你有無自由。不過你而家都無……仲要人決你又決。

忠： 返團契溝女！俾人知道好衰架。

寬： 衰得過你！你同阿God好熟咩？仲捉埋我隻手嚟舉。

忠： 何倚雯一直都望住你架！

寬： 唔係佢一直望住我，係你一直望住佢……

忠： 喂…咁個個都講你唔講……啲人咪諗……你唔中意阿God返團契做咩？

寬： 我唔返團契點知同阿God friend唔倒呀，你都傻架。

（寬在飲酒。）

KUAN	Dozens of people together with the lights off, everyone taking turns with their testimonies. Afterwards, everyone dribbled wax. They were crying like it was a slaughter. He Yi Wen, she... Oh my god... She went on for 15 minutes, like she was possessed. She balled her eyes out. Wow! Sniffling and saying, "Lord, I have given myself to you..." Honestly, it really was "oh my god". After those 15 minutes, I was sure that my god and her god weren't friends. And that she and I would never be friends either.
ZHONG	You don't have to believe. But let others have their freedom of religion.
KUAN	If you were with her... you think you'd be free? But you're not free now either... You just joined the confirmation because everyone else was doing it.
ZHONG	Chasing chicks at the fellowship. That's horrible.
KUAN	It's still better than you. And you are so close with God? You even volunteered me!
ZHONG	He Yi Wen was always looking at you.
KUAN	It wasn't that she was always looking me. It was that you were always looking at her.
ZHONG	Hey! Everybody was saying the same things. If you didn't say the same things, they got suspicious about your being at fellowship.
KUAN	How would I know that God and I couldn't be friends unless I joined the fellowship? Stupid!

(*Kuan drinks.*)

忠：　嗰晚唔係你撳住我，就唔駛三個月之後至追倒何倚雯。

寬：　你唔留返佢啲嘢，就唔駛有今晚囉。

忠：　⋯⋯我都話我中意回味個下咯！

寬：　你應該擺喺阿媽度，間唔中返去懷緬下咪算囉。

忠：　唉⋯⋯如果初戀可以擺喺最後你話幾好呢。

　　（忠飲酒。）

寬：　總之喺而家個女人面前，你要對以前啲嘢全部話「唔記得」，同佢嗰啲嘢呢，就算唔記得你都要扮記得。「哦！個次吖嗎，係啦，嗰日⋯⋯我緊係記得啦。」

忠：　「嘩，個次真係⋯⋯嘩⋯⋯點會唔記得呀⋯⋯」。OK，「咩要記得，咩要唔記得，記得嘅唔記得，唔記得嘅要記得。」

寬：　咁就乜撚嘢都得。

　　（兩人笑，飲酒。）

忠：　記得喇。（醉了）有啲嘢喺哩度（指著心）你係抹唔甩架⋯⋯

　　（舞台另一邊出現一殯儀館職員的聲音。）

職：　（場外大聲地）黎材友！

　　（寬望向聲音傳來的這一邊。）

職：　喺你邊個呀？

寬：　（有點恍惚）⋯⋯我老竇⋯⋯

ZHONG If you hadn't stopped me that night, it wouldn't have taken me three months to bag He Yi Wen.

KUAN If you hadn't kept her things, you wouldn't be here tonight.

ZHONG … I said I like to think about it once in a while!

KUAN You should have kept them at your mother's. Think about it at her place.

(*Zhong drinks.*)

KUAN You have to "forget" everything in the past for the woman you have now. And for this woman, you have to pretend to remember, even if you forget. "Oh, that time? Yes, that day… Of course I remember."

ZHONG "Wow, that time was… wow… How could I forget…" OK, "Remember everything. Forget everything. Forget what you remembered. Remember what you forgot."

KUAN Then you'll be fucking great.

(*They laugh and drink.*)

ZHONG Oh yes… (*Drunk.*) There are some things (*Points at heart*) you can't wipe away…

(*The voice of the funeral parlor employee comes from another side of the stage.*)

EMPLOYEE (*Loudly from offstage*) Li Cai You!

(*Kuan looks in the direction of the voice.*)

EMPLOYEE What is the relation?

KUAN (*A little confused.*) … My dad…

忠： （*突然醒了*）喂……sorry，我唔係想煩你架…

寬： （*回過來*）無嘢！

忠： 揸揸水先。

　　　　（*忠起身離開。*）

　　　　（*舞台另一邊再出現一殯儀館職員的聲音。*）

職： （*場外大聲地*）係咪黎材友呀？

　　　　（*寬再望向聲音傳來的這一邊。*）

寬： 係呀。

　　　　（*寬起身行至櫃台前。*）

　　　　（*接下場。*）

ZHONG   (*Wakes up suddenly.*) Hey… Sorry. I didn't want to bother you…

KUAN   (*Returns.*) It's fine.

ZHONG   Gotta wee.

(*Zhong gets up.*)

(*The voice of the funeral parlor employee is heard from the other side of the stage.*)

EMPLOYEE   (*Loudly from offstage*) Is it Li Cai You?

(*Kuan looks towards the direction of the voice again.*)

KUAN   Yes.

(*Kuan rises and approaches the reception desk.*)

(*Next scene follows.*)

第七場：殯儀館一角

（*寬站在櫃台前。*）

職： （*場外*）你幾多號出殯？

寬： 我？

（*短暫停頓。*）

職： （*場外*）你嚟接嗰個！你老竇呀？

寬： （*有點不自在*）骨灰紙上面有寫架，三月十二。

（*一會後。殯儀館職員拿著一袋東西出來，邊行邊説。*）

職： 唉！喺埋便，俾人遮住咗。黎材友吖嗎？佢就係嘞。咁快你就買倒位喇！

寬： 私人嗰啲。

職： 係呀，將軍澳早就滿晒，柴灣又無。政府唔好淨係掛住賣地賺錢得架，遲吓嗰啲仲有排等呀。嗱，我話應該好似居屋咁，五年就可以自由買賣，補地價囉。實大把人放出嚟。俾個機會人哋上車吖嗎，啱唔啱先！咁嗰啲擺返屋企又一家團聚咯，咪好囉。做人父母都想在生嘅搵多個錢架。你話係咪！你可以同佢走嘞！

SCENE 7 – A CORNER OF THE FUNERAL PARLOR

(*Kuan stands in front of the reception desk.*)

EMPLOYEE (*From offstage*) What date is your funeral?

KUAN My funeral?

(*Short pause.*)

EMPLOYEE (*From offstage*) The one you are picking up. Your father!

KUAN (*Uncomfortably*) It says on the cremation certificate. March 12.

(*A moment. Funeral parlor employee brings out a cloth bag and speaks at the same time.*)

EMPLOYEE (*Sighs.*) Over here. It was blocked by someone. Li Cai You, right? Here he is. You managed to find a plot so fast!

KUAN It's a private plot.

EMPLOYEE Oh yes. Everything at Tseung Kwan O is full. There is nothing at Chai Wan either. The government shouldn't just concentrate on selling land to make money. The longer we wait, the longer the others will have to wait. I think it should be run like public housing, where you are free to sell it after five years. You get compensated when it sells. I bet lots of people would sell. You gotta give others a chance to rest. Right? Some can go home with their families. It's a good thing. Everyone wants to make a little more while they're still alive. Right? You can leave with him now.

寬：　　　吓？

（職員不回答。把袋東西隨手放上，寬即檢查袋上的名字。）

寬：　　　唔該。

職：　　　係度簽返。要唔要膠袋呀？

寬：　　　吓？

職：　　　五毫子！

寬：　　　吓？

職：　　　環保呀！

寬：　　　好呀！

職：　　　五毫子。

（職員拿膠袋。寬簽名。）

寬：　　　唔該。

（寬把布袋慢慢放入膠袋，用手抽著膠袋就如購物回家一樣離開。他停了一會，轉身。）

（燈光轉變。）

（寬把布袋從膠袋拿出來，看著，又把它放回去，又靜靜的抽著膠袋站住。寬停下來望住膠袋。）

KUAN   Huh?

            (*Funeral parlor employee does not answer. Puts the cloth bag down casually. Kuan examines the name on the bag.*)

KUAN   Thank you.

EMPLOYEE   Sign here. Do you want a bag?

KUAN   Huh?

EMPLOYEE   50 cents.

KUAN   Huh?

EMPLOYEE   Recycling.

KUAN   OK.

EMPLOYEE   50 cents.

            (*Employee gets a plastic bag. Kuan signs.*)

KUAN   Thanks.

            (*Kuan puts the cloth bag slowly into the plastic bag. He carries the plastic bag like a shopping bag and leaves. He stops for a moment. Turns around.*

            (*Lights change.*)

            (*Kuan takes out the cloth bag from the plastic bag, looks at it, and replaces it in the plastic bag. He stands quietly with the plastic bag. He continues to look at the bag.*)

寬：　有一次，我好細個嗰陣，七歲八歲倒，我哋去完街返屋企，佢拖住我行。我見到一檔賣魚蛋墨魚嘅車仔檔，我問爸爸：「我想食魚蛋」，佢話：「返去食飯仲食魚蛋」，我就「leu」佢要買：「一串啦兩粒之嗎」。佢就俾一毫子我，我好開心，結果我唔買魚蛋，我買咗一毫子墨魚，橙色嗰啲。我好開心，嗰條墨魚鬚仲好長。我揸住串墨魚，望過去我老竇嗰便，我好開心咁走返去佢度。我太開心⋯⋯走得好快⋯⋯結果震震下嗰墨魚震到跌咗落地下！我呆咗！我望住地下條墨魚，跟住又望一望我老竇。佢又望住我，我唔知點好，嗰吓我直頭想執返佢嚟食。揸住支簽但係無得食，我想喊都喊唔出。我行埋老豆度，我話：「爸爸跌咗呀」。我好想佢會俾多一毫子我買過另一串，不過佢無，佢仲用隻手「撩」下我個嘴，話：「無得食lu，走咁快做乜啫」。我知佢話過只係買一串。只係一串！

（靜。）

寬：　佢拖返我隻手就行，我另一隻手仲揸住支簽⋯⋯我真係好唔開心⋯⋯「無咗」！

（此場完。）

KUAN   Once, when I was very little, about 7 or 8, we were walking home. He held my hand as we walked. I saw a hawker selling fish balls and squid. I told dad, "I want to eat some fish balls." He said, "We'll have dinner when we get home." I nagged him to buy fish balls for me, "Just one skewer. Only two pieces." He gave me 10 cents. I was very happy, but I didn't buy fish balls. I bought 10 cents worth of squid, the orange kind. I was really happy. The tentacles on the squid were very long. I carried the skewer of squid, and I looked over at my dad. I started walking carefully back to him. But I was too excited… I began to run… and the squid fell off the skewer. I was shocked. I stared at the squid on the ground, and then I looked at my dad. He looked at me. I didn't know what to do. I wanted to pick up the squid and eat it at that moment. I had a skewer in my hand but no food. I wanted to cry, but nothing came out. I walked over to my dad. I said, "It fell, dad." I wanted him to give me another 10 cents to buy some more, but he didn't. He just used his finger and teased my mouth, "Shouldn't have run. No more now." I knew he said he'd only by one skewer. Just one skewer.

(Silence.)

KUAN   He held my hand and we continued to walk. The skewer was in my other hand… I was so disappointed… "No more."

(End of scene.)

第八場：寬媽家中

(*琪在講電話，一面整理膠台布和擺筷子。*)

琪：　　（*對電話*）唔駛等你呀？你又話今日會早！

　　　　（*琪收線，不悅。*）

　　　　（*媽從廚房出。*）

媽：　　返到未呀，到我就煮魚啦？唔係又等……邊好食！

琪：　　唔駛等㗎！叫我哋自己食先。

媽：　　又話八點，次次都係咁。唔得就唔好話返嚟食啦。

琪：　　不如我哋食啦，唔等佢喇。

媽：　　咁我煮埋條魚。

琪：　　伯母呀，唔好煮魚喇，三個人點食咁多啫……

　　　　（*邊入廚房邊説。*）

媽：　　唔好，煮埋啦，仲有排骨都未炒……

琪：　　有菜有豉油雞咪得囉，又有湯！

　　　　（*媽出拿著菜和一個隔油湯壺放下。*）

媽：　　你食吖嘛！

琪：　　我食唔到咁多嘢……

媽：　　吓？

SCENE 8 – KUAN'S MOTHER'S HOME

(*Qi is talking on the phone as she places chopsticks and a plastic cover on the table.*)

QI   (*Into phone.*) Don't wait for you? I thought you said you'd be early today.

(*Qi hangs up. Unhappy.*)

(*Mother enters from kitchen.*)

MOTHER   Is he home yet? If he is, I'll cook the fish. It's no good if it's cold.

QI   He said not to wait. He told us to eat first.

MOTHER   He said eight o'clock. It's the same every time. If he can't make it he shouldn't have said he'd come back for dinner.

QI   Let's not wait. Let's eat.

MOTHER   Then let me cook the fish.

QI   Auntie, don't bother. It's too much food for three…

(*She exits to the kitchen.*)

MOTHER   No, I'll cook it. I still have to cook the spare ribs…

QI   We have vegetables, chicken and soup.

(*Mother re-enters with vegetables and a jug of soup.*)

MOTHER   You'll eat it, right?

QI   I can't eat that much…

MOTHER   Huh?

琪：　　　排骨都唔好炒喇。就咁得啦。

媽：　　　咁……飲湯啦！

琪：　　　好吖。我飲湯先。

（*琪入廚房邊説。*）

琪：　　　我幫你擺左條魚入雪櫃，隻雞我挾起一半俾阿寬吖！

（*媽靜靜坐下。*）

（*琪出拿雞放下，二人飲湯，靜。*）

媽：　　　咁一陣帶壺返去。

琪：　　　唔好喇，我聽日飛呀，飲唔到費事嘥埋。留俾阿寬飲呀！

媽：　　　聽朝飲埋佢囉，帶上飛機。攞壺返去。

琪：　　　水唔上得機架……

媽：　　　係咩……哦……

琪：　　　……都好吖……我聽朝飲吖。

（*靜。*）

媽：　　　你近排都好少上嚟食飯。

琪：　　　阿寬又忙，一係我又飛咗。

琪：　　　其實我都有湯飲架。

媽：　　　你識煲咩，你？

琪：　　　返阿媽度咪有囉。

媽：　　　你一個月返唔倒幾多次啦！

QI   Don't make the spare ribs. It's enough.

MOTHER Then let's have soup first.

QI   OK. I'll drink the soup first.

(*Qi speaks as she exits into the kitchen.*)

QI   I'll put the fish back into the fridge. I'll save half the chicken for Kuan.

(*Mother sits quietly.*)

(*Qi re-enters with chicken. They both drink soup. Silence.*)

MOTHER You should take some home for later.

QI   Oh no. I have to fly tomorrow. I don't want to waste it. Save it for Kuan.

MOTHER You can drink it in the morning. Take it on the plane. Take some home.

QI   I can't bring liquid onto the plane…

MOTHER Oh, really?

QI   OK, I'll drink some tomorrow morning.

(*Silence.*)

MOTHER You haven't come by for dinner much lately.

QI   Kuan is very busy and I've been flying.

QI   Actually, I like to drink soup too.

MOTHER You know how to make soup?

QI   When I go back to my mother's.

MOTHER How many times a month do you get to go back?

琪： 唔係，都有一兩次飛溫哥華架嗎，咪返屋企住囉，長途唔係個個好似我咁肯飛架。唔係阿媽都唔肯過我！

媽： 嗰邊淨得啲雪藏嘢，煲湯要新鮮雞至好架。

琪： 唔係架，唐人街乜都有，香港啲嘢都唔夠嗰邊好食……

媽： 係咩……

琪： 不過都有好多嘢係香港好啲。

（靜。）

媽： 你阿爸阿媽點會肯俾你自己喺香港架呢！

琪： 好悶架嗰邊……得啦，細佬又喺佢哋身邊，總之我而家最好又可以成日返去俾佢哋見下咪得囉。又有你啲湯飲，OK啦，總之阿寬唔返我都嚟食飯咪得囉。你唔好話我成日黐餐就得喇。

媽： 傻咩，你日日嚟都得！以前阿寬就真係少返嚟食，而家你哋返多咗囉。不過你哋要做嘢吖嗎，我成日都係一個架啦，有乜所謂啫。

琪： 好吖，我唔飛就上嚟啦！嚟吖，食雞吖。

媽： 你食啦，我唔食！

琪： 係喎！

| QI | Oh, I get to go to Vancouver once or twice a month. I stay at home. Not everyone is willing to fly long haul flights like me. But otherwise, my mother wouldn't have it. |

MOTHER   They only have frozen food there. For soup, you need fresh chicken.

QI   No, they have everything in Chinatown. They have better food than Hong Kong.

MOTHER   Really?

QI   Of course, Hong Kong still has lots of advantages.

(*Silence.*)

MOTHER   How is it that your parents let you stay here in Hong Kong by yourself?

QI   It's so boring there… They're fine. My brother is with them over there. As long as I can go back once in a while, they're fine. I can drink your soup. OK. I can come to dinner even if Kuan doesn't come back. I hope you don't mind me inviting myself.

MOTHER   Don't be silly. You can come every day. Kuan didn't used to come home much. He comes more often now. But you both have to work. I'm by myself most of the time. No matter.

QI   OK. I'll come up if I'm not flying. Have some chicken.

MOTHER   You go ahead. I can't eat chicken.

QI   Oh right!

媽： 好彩你講起，唔係又唔記得……

（媽起身入內，拿了一個file出來。）

媽： 你幫我睇吓幾時覆診，又睇眼又骨科！你幫我睇吓邊日睇腫瘤科！

（媽拿出數張覆診紙，琪逐一地看。）

琪： 睇眼就要年尾十二月。嘩，有無搞錯呀？骨科要出年四月呀。腫瘤科就下個再下個星期三，廿三號上晝九點半。

媽： 好彩你提一提，唔係我都唔記得。廿三號。我係記得差唔多架喇。

琪： 有無人同你去呀，阿寬唔得我同你去吖。

媽： 唏，唔駛。喺埋你哋啲時間咩……又返工你哋。

琪： 有人同你去好啲，我唔係日日都要返嘅，得啦，我陪你去吖。

媽： 駛乜吖。到時你得閒先啦……以前就佢老竇一齊去！一去就去成日架，等又等幾個鐘，淨係攞藥都試過等兩個鐘呀，自己去得啦。

（寬開門入。）

媽： 返喇……一係又咁快……（*馬上倒一碗湯。*）

MOTHER I'm glad you mentioned it. Otherwise, I'd have forgotten again.

(*Mother exits and returns with a file.*)

MOTHER Help me check when my next appointment is. With both the optometrist and orthopedic surgeon. And check for me when my next appointment is with the oncologist.

(*Mother brings out several pieces of paper. Qi examines them.*)

QI The optometrist is in December. Wow, are they kidding? The orthopedic surgeon is next April. The oncologist is in two weeks, on Wednesday, the 23rd at 9:30am.

MOTHER Good thing you reminded me. I almost forgot. The 23rd. I knew it was around that time.

QI Is anyone going with you? If Kuan can't go, I'll go with you.

MOTHER Oh, no need. I don't want to waste your time. You have to work.

QI It's better if someone goes with you. I don't work every day. It's fine. I'll go with you.

MOTHER No need. Only if you're free... His father used to go with me. It's a whole day's trip. We wait for hours. Once we waited for two hours just for the medication. I'll go by myself.

(*Kuan enters.*)

MOTHER You're home... So soon... (*Immediately brings a bowl of soup.*)

寬： 食緊嘩，食啦。（*入了房。*）

媽： 飲湯先啦（*再入廚房。*）我去整埋條魚。

琪： （*琪跟到房前*）又話打電話返嚟……

媽： （*從內大聲地*）煮埋啲排骨啦。

琪： （*大聲向房*）你食唔食排骨呀？

寬： （*從內*）吓？是但啦……

（*靜，琪一人坐著不動，突然向廚房。*）

琪： 唔好煮排骨啦，伯母，魚都唔好啦。

媽： （*從內*）唔煮？

琪： （*大聲地*）唔好煮喇，佢唔食喇。

（*寬出現，琪靜下來坐著，寬邊行邊說坐下，邊飲湯。*）

寬： 個客都"short"架，諗倒啲屎忽嘢又要從頭搞過，色版又要改，圖又要改，娘到爆佢哋嘅，都唔知點解會好似係佢個啲至啱咁，cheap，「低檔次貨色」咪做啲低檔次貨囉。蕉皮！仲話聽日要改晒啲圖俾佢睇，唔駛瞓呀！我話要改你改囉，叫晒班靚放工，「pat」低就走。（*飲完湯，停，寬望琪*）做咩，好快架喇喝我。仆到咁返嚟架喇。

KUAN	You're already eating? Go ahead, eat. (*Exits to his bedroom.*)
MOTHER	Drink soup first. (*Exits to kitchen.*) I'll make the fish.
QI	(*Qi follows to bedroom door.*) You said you'd call…
MOTHER	(*From inside, loudly*) Let me cook the ribs, too.
QI	(*Shouting towards the bedroom*) Do you want ribs?
KUAN	(*From inside*) Huh? Yeah, whatever…
	(*Silence. Qi sits motionless.*)
QI	(*Suddenly, towards the kitchen*) Don't cook the spare ribs, auntie. Don't cook the fish either.
MOTHER	(*From inside*) No?
QI	(*Loudly*) No, don't cook them. He doesn't want them.
	(*Kuan appears. Qi sits quietly. Drinking soup, Kuan walks in and sits down*)
KUAN	(*Still drinking soup.*) That client is nuts. He thinks up the dumbest plan possible, and then starts all over again. He wants to change the colour, he wants to change the plan. Son of a bitch. Only his ideas are good enough. So cheap. He wants cheap, second-class work. Fine, so I give him second-class stuff. Asshole! And he wants all the changes by tomorrow. Hello? Sleep? You want changes? You change them. I told the whole team to drop everything and go home. (*Finishes soup. Stops. Looks at Qi.*) What? I got here as fast as I could. I raced all the way.

琪： 食唔食排骨呀，唔食就叫你阿媽唔好煮喇。

寬： 是但啦，煮咗咪食囉。

琪： ⋯⋯

寬： 食完飯同你返去⋯⋯

琪： 我聽日早call！

寬： 你要飛咩？

琪： 係呀！飛加拿大！

寬： 駛唔駛聽朝同你去機場！你聽日幾點call呀？

琪： （冷淡地）你聽日要交過晒啲圖呀。

寬： ⋯⋯我聽日實唔交⋯⋯

琪： 我好早呀，自己call的士⋯⋯

寬： 是但囉。咁一陣同你返去。成個幾禮拜無上你度啦！食完飯就走啦。

琪： 返去做乜，我要早啲瞓⋯⋯

寬： ⋯⋯咁起碼都送你返去吖嗎！

琪： 送我返去咁又點呀？

寬： 咩點呀⋯⋯

（媽手持湯壺上。）

媽： 條魚蒸緊，好快就得。琪呀，壺湯裝好啦，一陣記得攞呀。

琪： 哦！

QI	Do you want spare ribs? If you don't, I'll tell your mom not to cook it.
KUAN	Whatever. I'll eat it if it's cooked.
QI	…
KUAN	I'll go home with you after we eat.
QI	I work early tomorrow.
KUAN	You're flying tomorrow?
QI	Yeah. Canada.
KUAN	You want me to go to the airport with you? What's your call time?
QI	(*Coolly*) You have to submit new designs tomorrow.
KUAN	I am not submitting any new designs tomorrow.
QI	It's early. I'll get a taxi.
KUAN	Whatever. Then I'll go home with you later. I haven't been to your place all week. Let's go after dinner.
QI	What for? I have to sleep early.
KUAN	… Then I'll take you home.
QI	So what if you take me home?
KUAN	What do you mean so what if?
	(*Mother enters with soup jug.*)
MOTHER	The fish is steaming. Will be ready soon. Qi, here's your jug of soup. Remember to take it home.
QI	OK.

媽： 你又話八點，等嚟等去。

寬： ……我想架咋……返咗嚟咪得囉，你唔好煮咁多吖嗎……是但啦……由佢囉食唔晒……

琪： 下個再下個禮拜三伯母要覆診，你同唔同倒佢去呀。

寬： 咩覆診？

媽： 腫瘤科。

寬： 吓……er ……好呀，我同你去吖。

媽： 唔駛。

琪： 你話得至好，唔係又是但得個講字。

寬： 咩呀？話得就得啦（挾雞給媽。）雞脾。

琪： 你阿媽唔食架！你好似唔知咁嘅！

寬： ……咩呀？

琪： 你咩都唔知？

寬： （突然大聲）我知！我下個禮拜同你去睇醫生！

琪： 下個再下個禮拜呀！

寬： 做咩啫……

媽： 哂，自己去，自己去就得。嚟啦，食飯，食晒啲餸，食唔倒就唔好食飯。條魚得喇。（媽入廚房。）

（二人不語，寬繼續食。）

（此場完。）

MOTHER	You said eight o'clock. We waited for you.
KUAN	Don't you think I wanted to be here on time?... I'm here now, right? Don't cook so much... Just whatever... Doesn't matter if we don't finish...
QI	Your mother has a doctor's appointment two weeks from Wednesday. Can you go with her?
KUAN	What appointment?
MOTHER	With the oncologist.
KUAN	Oh... um... yeah... I'll go with you.
MOTHER	You don't have to.
QI	Are you sure you can go? Don't say you can if you can't.
KUAN	What is this? I said I will go. (*Gets Mother a piece of chicken.*) Drumstick.
QI	Your mother can't eat chicken. You don't seem to know anything.
KUAN	What?
QI	You don't know anything.
KUAN	(*Suddenly loudly*) I do know! I'm going to the doctor with you next week.
QI	It's the week after next.
KUAN	What is it?
MOTHER	Shh... I'll go by myself. Come on, let's eat. Finish the food. Forget the rice. The fish is ready. (*Mother exits to kitchen.*)
	(*The two of them don't speak. Kuan continues to eat.*)
	(*End of scene.*)

第九場：醫院一角

（*姐和媽坐著，神情有點呆。寬趕至。*）

寬：　　媽呢？

姐：　　喺嗰邊！你下晝駛唔駛返去？

寬：　　唔係唔得，你要走嚒？

姐：　　係呀，最好你下晝陪住佢啦。又話今日同佢
　　　　嚟。我「格」硬唔返架啦今朝。

寬：　　得啦，點啫，咩啫？

姐：　　應該係復發呀。

寬：　　吓！肯定嚒。

姐：　　唔好咁大聲，費事佢聽到。

　　　　（*把寬推至一邊。*）

姐：　　唉，應該係。佢心口上面有粒嘢生咗出嚟。

寬：　　咁即係咩啫？

姐：　　個醫生而家就唔話肯定係，話要做個CT掃描，
　　　　睇咗報告至確診喎。

寬：　　係咪下晝做呀？

姐：　　喺呢度就要排到出年喎，最好自己去私家做。
　　　　姑娘幫我哋約緊，佢地轉介有六折。

寬：　　幾多都好啦。佢知唔知呀？

SCENE 9 – A CORNER IN THE HOSPITAL

(*Sister and Mother sit. They seem dazed. Kuan hurriedly enters.*)

KUAN　　　Where is mom?

SISTER　　Over there. Do you have to go back in the afternoon?

KUAN　　　I don't have to. You have to go?

SISTER　　Yeah. It's best you stay with her for the afternoon. You said you'd come with her today. I managed to get the morning off.

KUAN　　　Fine. Well? What is it?

SISTER　　I think it has come back.

KUAN　　　What? Really?

SISTER　　Keep your voice down. Don't let her hear you.

(*Pushes Kuan to one side.*)

SISTER　　(*Sighs.*) I think so. She has a lump on her breast.

KUAN　　　What does that mean?

SISTER　　The doctor hasn't confirmed. He said she needs another CT scan. He'll make his diagnosis after seeing the report.

KUAN　　　Is that this afternoon?

SISTER　　At this hospital, the wait is until next year. We have to go to a private hospital. The nurse is making an appointment for us. There is a 60% discount with their referral.

KUAN　　　Whatever it takes. Does she know?

姐：	知，醫生講嗰陣佢都喺度，不過就呆呆地。
	（*兩人靜。寬坐在媽身旁。*）
媽：	食飯未呀？成點咯！
寬：	未呀……
媽：	一陣要唔要返返工呀。要就食飯先。
寬：	唔食住喇……你肚唔肚餓呀，買啲嘢俾你食吖？
姐：	你食咩，叫阿寬去買吖。
媽：	我唔餓，你哋去食啦，又要返工。
寬：	得喇。
	（*頓。*）
媽：	醫生講咗喇。
寬：	……唔一定係嘅，醫生都未證實。或者無事呢。
媽：	（*煩躁地*）做乜咁耐架。
姐：	姑娘打電話去約，要問下邊間有期，想下個禮拜約埋返嚟覆診。
媽：	阿寬你下晝唔返同我去銀行攞錢，要成萬蚊。
寬：	駛乜呀！下星期先去照，我有呀。
	（*靜。*）

SISTER	Yes. She was there when the doctor told me. But she was numb.
	(*They are silent. Kuan sits next to his mother.*)
MOTHER	Have you had lunch? It's nearly one.
KUAN	No…
MOTHER	Do you have to go back to work? If you do, then go and eat first.
KUAN	No… Are you hungry? I'll get you a bite to eat.
SISTER	What do you want? I'll go and buy something.
MOTHER	I'm not hungry. You two go and eat. You have to work.
KUAN	It's fine.
	(*A moment.*)
MOTHER	The doctor said it.
KUAN	It's not for sure. He hasn't made his diagnosis. Maybe it's nothing.
MOTHER	(*Annoyed*) Why is it taking so long?
SISTER	The nurse is making an appointment. She has to find out which hospital has an opening. Then she has to make a follow-up appointment for next week.
MOTHER	Kuan, if you're not going back to work in the afternoon, come to the bank with me. This will take over $10,000.
KUAN	That's all right. The scan is next week. I have some money.
	(*Silence.*)

姐： 　　我入去問下姑娘得未。

　　　　　（*姐離開。*）

媽： 　　我以為捱咗一刀就無事。

　　　　　（*媽把頭挨在寬的肩膊上，望著前方。*）

　　　　　（*此場完。*）

SISTER   I'll go and ask the nurse.

          (*Sister exits.*)

MOTHER   I thought one cut would be enough.

          (*Mother places her head on Kuan's shoulder and looks straight ahead.*)

          (*End of scene.*)

第十場：琪的家

（寬一人坐在屋內沒有開燈，傳來開門聲。琪穿著空姐的制服出現，帶著行李箱和洗衣店的一袋衣服。一面講著手電，非常開心的樣子。不知寬在屋內。也沒有開燈。）

琪：　　如果你等得咪等囉……如果有架車停喺佢門口兩個禮拜，你估我阿媽見唔見到你呢……搵FBI拉你架。又係嗰FBI係美國架呵…咁你喺度等囉，兩個禮拜啫。

（琪已把行李安置在大門前。入廚房拿著水杯出，一面飲水一面講。）

琪：　　我個籮柚仲有啲痛呀，隻手仲軟緊呀，連洗衣舖袋衫都無力攞呀…係呀，底衫褲我都攞出街洗架……關你咩事啫……哈哈……再去吖……好……

（琪到沙發前才看見寬，兩人望著對方，停了一刻。）

琪：　　喂，唔講喇……你電話費貴呀……talk to you later, OK ... Bye。做乜唔開燈，玩驚喜呀。

（琪開燈。）

SCENE 10 – QI'S HOME

(*Kuan sits alone inside the house. The lights are off. You hear the sound of the door opening. Qi enters wearing her flight attendant uniform, carrying luggage and clothes from the cleaners. She is talking on her mobile phone. She seems happy. She doesn't know Kuan is inside and does not turn on the lights.*)

QI Go ahead and wait if you want… If you parked your car outside my mom's house for two weeks, don't you think she'd see you… We'll call the FBI. Oh right. They're American… Then you'll just have to wait. It's just two weeks.

(*Qi has dropped her luggage at the door. She enters the kitchen to get a drink of water. She speaks as she drinks.*)

QI My ass hurts and my arm is sore. I can't even pick up my laundry… Yeah, I get my underwear professionally cleaned… None of your business… Haha… Go again?… OK…

(*Qi approaches the sofa and sees Kuan. They see each other. Pause.*)

QI Hey, I can't talk now… Phone bills are expensive… Talk to you later. OK… Bye. Why didn't you turn on the lights? You want to scare me to death?

(*Qi turns on the lights.*)

寬：　　　係呀。

琪：　　　今日早收呀？八點幾咋喎，早收唔返去同阿媽食飯。

寬：　　　阿媽去咗家姐度。

琪：　　　好彩我早返黎啫，原本啲同事話去打邊爐架……

寬：　　　你而家去囉。

琪：　　　唔好！做咩你……

寬：　　　做咩……無咩呀……

琪：　　　攬下我，我想你攬下我。

（站在沙發前向著寬，把雙手打開等待著，但寬坐著不動望著琪。）

琪：　　　咁樣唔係好高要求啫。你知唔知我今日幾辛苦呀！已經爆到唔爆，仲要成幾十個中學生，淨係沖杯麵都手軟。

（靜。）

琪：　　　返到嚟你好似咩都無發生過咁！

寬：　　　你無打電話俾我！

琪：　　　你都無打俾我呀。

寬：　　　你隻手好痛咩？

琪：　　　咪講咗囉……仲有三個BB仔……

寬：　　　簕柚「燉」親呀？

琪：　　　唔係呀！

寬：　　　你又同人講你好痛？

KUAN   Yeah.

QI   You got off early today? It's only eight. Why don't you eat dinner with your mother?

KUAN   Mom is at my sister's house.

QI   Good thing I came back early. My colleagues wanted to go for hot pot dinner...

KUAN   You can go now.

QI   No! What's wrong...

KUAN   What's wrong? Nothing.

QI   Hold me. I want you to hold me.

        (*Stands in front of Kuan on the sofa, spreads out her arms and waits. But Kuan sits motionless.*)

QI   That's not asking for too much. I had a hard day today. The flight was packed. And there were a dozen or so high school kids. I am exhausted from making instant noodles.

        (*Silence.*)

QI   You act as if I don't exist.

KUAN   You didn't call me.

QI   You didn't call me either.

KUAN   Your arm hurts?

QI   I told you... And there were three babies...

KUAN   You fell on your ass?

QI   No!

KUAN   Then why did you tell him your ass hurts?

琪：　　　我同啲 friend去咗騎馬之嘛！

寬：　　　咁咪幾好玩。

（*靜。*）

琪：　　　我沖個涼！

寬：　　　騎完馬梗係劫啦。

（*寬突然捉住琪，強吻她。*）

琪：　　　唔好呀，我好劫呀。

（*寬暴力地攬住琪再強吻她，把琪推落沙發，
兩人瘋狂的糾纏起來。*）

琪：　　　唔好呀……（*大叫*）唔好呀……

（*寬不理她，繼續強行，最後琪掌摑寬幾下他
才停下來。*）

琪：　　　你痴線架你。

寬：　　　你依家咁算點呀！

琪：　　　痴線架你！你發咩癲呀……你返屋企，你今晚
唔好喺度。

寬：　　　你有冇理過我呀？

琪：　　　你竟然問我呢個問題！

寬：　　　點解呀？

琪：　　　咩點解呀！

寬：　　　我點呀？

琪：　　　我都想問你呀！你中意就嚟，唔中意就理都唔
理，你點解呀？

QI	I went horseback riding with my friends.
KUAN	That sounds like fun.
	(*Silence.*)
QI	I'm taking a bath.
KUAN	Must be tired after horseback riding.
	(*Kuan suddenly grabs Qi and kisses her forcibly.*)
QI	Don't. I'm tired.
	(*Kuan roughly holds onto Qi and forces his kisses on her. He pushes Qi onto the sofa. The two of them struggle crazily.*)
QI	Don't... (*Screams*) Stop!
	(*Kuan ignores her and continues forcibly. Finally Qi slaps Kuan a few times before he stops.*)
QI	Have you gone crazy?
KUAN	What the hell do you want?
QI	You're crazy. What the hell is wrong with you. Go home. Don't stay here tonight.
KUAN	Don't you care about me?
QI	How can you ask me that?
KUAN	Why?
QI	What do you mean why?
KUAN	What about me?
QI	I want to ask you the same thing. You come as you like, go as you please. What's wrong with you?

寬： 我唔理咩？

琪： 我問你點解呀，（大聲）點解吖？

寬： 我乜嘢無理呀？

琪： 你要返屋企吖嗎！你要睇住阿媽吖嗎？仲要返大陸吖嗎？

寬： 講我阿媽咩呀，佢成日一個人喺屋企，我係咪要返去呀？

琪： 我都一個人喺屋企呀！

寬： 咁點同啫。

琪： 係囉！我係你邊個呀！咩嘢都唔係！我成日諗我係咪真係咁唔值錢呀。我不如返加拿大仲有daddy mummy錫我呀。唔駛就咁俾人擺係度。

寬： 點樣擺係度，你又成日飛，我咪返去囉。

琪： 一個又係咁擺，兩個又係咁擺，仲有第三個。

寬： 咩第三個呀！

琪： 大陸嗰個！

寬： 大陸邊個？

琪： 打嚟搵你嗰個。

寬： 邊個呀！

琪： 係邊個你自己知，你成日返上去我都唔知你搵邊個，邊個就邊個啦。總之我唔覺得我喺你心目中好重要。

寬： 痴線……個個都痴線。

KUAN   Don't you think I care?

QI   I want to ask you why. (*Loudly*) Why?

KUAN   What do you mean I don't care?

QI   You need to go home, right? Need to take care of your mom, right? Need to go to China, right?

KUAN   What about my mother? She's home alone all day. Why shouldn't I see her?

QI   I live alone too.

KUAN   That's different.

QI   That's right. Who am I to you? Nothing. I keep asking myself, am I worth so little? Why don't I go back to my mom and dad in Canada. They love me. I don't need to sit here by myself.

KUAN   What do you mean sit here by yourself? You fly all the time. So I go back.

QI   The first one can sit. The second one can sit. And so can the third one.

KUAN   What do you mean the third one?

QI   The one in China!

KUAN   Which one in China?

QI   The one who called for you.

KUAN   Who?

QI   You know what I'm talking about. You're up in China all the time. I don't know who you see up there and I don't care. I just don't feel I'm important to you.

KUAN   You're crazy… You're all crazy.

琪：　　　是但啦！我多手睇你電話啫。

寬：　　　我電話？我電話邊有啲邊個呀。（狂亂地拿出電話以示清白）

琪：　　　依家冇，之前有呀。

寬：　　　（大叫）唔係。OK，總之冇。而家冇！

琪：　　　（更大叫）有！你有！你啲friend都話你有。

寬：　　　邊個friend呀？！（停頓）……無喇依家。

琪：　　　有冇都好喇，OK。

寬：　　　OK……OK。我中意你㗎OK！

琪：　　　你爸爸唔喺度我唔想煩你，我早就知。不過都唔關事。你對屋企人是但，對我又係是但。你就算返去又點呀，你真係有理佢咩！你咪又係擺佢係度就算。你最叻㗎啦，食又得，唔食又得，總之擺係度咪得囉。

　　　　　（靜。）

寬：　　　我知你好劫，我哋今晚唔講喇好冇。

琪：　　　我要你攬吓我你都無反應。

寬：　　　唔係呀……

琪：　　　或者你無諗過我哋會點，我屋企喺半個地球咁遠，我唔係淨係因為貪玩留係度。

QI   Whatever! I saw it on your phone.

KUAN   My phone? Who was on my phone? (*Wildly retrieves his phone to prove his innocence.*)

QI   Not right now. Before.

KUAN   (*Loudly.*) No. Look, there's nothing. Nothing now.

QI   (*Louder.*) Yes, there is. You've got someone. Your friends say you do.

KUAN   Which friend? (*Stops.*) There is no one now.

QI   I don't care, OK?

KUAN   OK… OK… I love you, OK?

QI   Your father passed away and I didn't want to bother you. But I knew a while back. That doesn't matter. You are nonchalant about your family. You're nonchalant about me. So what if you go to her? Do you care about her? You want her to sit there. That's what you do best. Eat, or not eat. You just want her to sit there.

          (*Silence.*)

KUAN   I know you're tired. Let's not talk about it anymore tonight, all right?

QI   I just want you to hold me, and you give me nothing.

KUAN   No…

QI   Maybe you never thought about what would happen to us. My home is half way around the world. I didn't stay here for fun.

寬：　　　好耐之前架啦……

琪：　　　是但啦。……我同班朋友一齊去騎馬啫，我無
　　　　　同第二個一齊。佢要點我唔理。不過你有自由
　　　　　我都有自由。如果令你誤會唔sorry。

寬：　　　琪……

琪：　　　或者我哋分開啦……你搵邊個都得。陪多啲阿
　　　　　媽囉！我唔係你阿媽煮嗰啲餸，你食又得唔食
　　　　　又得。我地分開啦。

寬：　　　……琪……

琪：　　　你返去啦！

　　　　　（*寬沒有離開，反而坐在沙發上。*）

琪：　　　我唔要你喺度呀。

　　　　　（*寬垂下頭不望琪，突然大聲地。*）

寬：　　　做咩呀而家……

　　　　　（*此場完。*）

KUAN   It was a long time ago...

QI   Whatever... I just went horseback riding with some friends. I wasn't with someone else. I don't care what he wants. But you are free and so am I. If I have misled you, I'm sorry.

KUAN   Qi...

QI   Maybe we should separate... You can see whoever you want. Spend more time with your mother. I'm not like those dishes your mother cooks. You can eat or not eat them. Let's stop seeing each other.

KUAN   Qi...

QI   Go home.

        (*Kuan doesn't leave. He sits on the sofa instead.*)

QI   I don't want you here.

KUAN   What's going on?

        (*End of scene.*)

第十一場

（音樂出現，天空的星星閃耀著。）

（寬在街上獨自徘徊著，飲著酒。直至他醉倒了，燈光照在他身上。）

（舞台的一角燈亮，媽坐在廳中一人。）

（舞台另一角燈亮，忠在玩著嬰兒玩具。）

（舞台另一角燈亮，姐在講著手提電話。）

（舞台另一角燈亮，大口似是在服食精神科藥物。）

（最後他突然寬醒來，星星、音樂和他身上的燈光同時消失。）

（此場完。）

SCENE 11

(*Music appears. Stars sparkle in the sky.*)

(*Kuan is wandering alone on the streets, drinking until he is drunk. Light shines on him.*)

(*Light appears in one corner of the stage. Mother is sitting in the living room alone.*)

(*Light appears in another corner of the stage. Zhong is playing with baby toys.*)

(*Light appears in another corner of the stage. Sister is speaking on her mobile phone.*)

(*Light appears in another corner of the stage. Da Kou appears to be taking medication for mental illness.*)

(*Kuan suddenly awakes. The stars, music and the light on him disappear simultaneously.*

(*End of scene.*)

第十二場：大口的家

（寬在廳中醒過來，大口出現。）

大：　　醒啦。

寬：　　（嘗試醒過來）……嘩……

大：　　成支 Black「隊」晒，好high喎尋晚。

寬：　　我幾時上咗嚟……件衫呢？

大：　　你話呢！個的士佬呀上車就依依牙牙媽媽聲
　　　　話……「今晚真好彩，執支咁嘅旗，實要洗
　　　　餐死又乜又七咁」……我屌尻佢囉，「收皮啦
　　　　你……有個膠袋咪得囉」，佢話同我賭五舊水
　　　　你實嘔倒成車係，我話「好呀，真係嘔出嚟
　　　　我俾五舊水你洗車囉，但係如果無整污糟你架
　　　　車，我俾五千蚊你同我飲撚晒袋嘢佢吖」。你
　　　　又係……揸到個膠袋咁實又唔嘔，諗住睇佢點
　　　　舐你袋嘢家嘛，你又幫我慳返。其實你又唔駛
　　　　咁堅持家嘛。我有喎！

寬：　　零印象呀，斷咗片。

大：　　不過一落車你就狂嘔。「pat」嘢就係大門口，
　　　　你一陣落倒樓自己去睇吓。

寬：　　唉，好痛個頭。

大：　　攞條熱毛巾俾你吖。（入內）

SCENE 12 – DA KOU'S HOME

(*Kuan wakes up in the living room. Da Kou appears.*)

DA   You're up.

KUAN   (*Tries to get up.*) … Wow…

DA   You drank an entire bottle of Black Label. Some night last night.

KUAN   When did I come up here?… Where's my shirt?

DA   Where do you think? The taxi driver was already bitching when you got in the cab… "My lucky night, running into your type. I'm gonna have to wash my cab inside and out. Blah blah blah…" Fuck him. "Shut the fuck up. We got a plastic bag." He made a bet with me for $500 that you'd puke inside the cab. I said, "Fine. If he upchucks I will give you $500 to clean your cab. But if he doesn't mess up your cab, I will give you $5,000 to eat everything he upchucks." Damn you. You had the bag tight in your hands, why didn't you puke? I wanted to see how he was gonna lick your puke. And you went and saved me the cash. You shouldn't have held back. I can afford it.

KUAN   No impression. The video reel is broken.

DA   You puked the moment you got out of the cab, right in front of the door. When you leave here you can see for yourself.

KUAN   Ow. My head hurts.

DA   I'll get you a hot towel. (*Exits.*)

寬：　　　唔該……嘩……頂你個肺吖……（摸頭）

大：　　　（從內大聲）喂，阿琪打鑼咁搵你呀……

寬：　　　吓……佢搵我……

大：　　　佢打到嚟呢度刮你呀……（大口出）

寬：　　　你唔叫醒我……

大：　　　（把毛巾遞給寬）第一，你條粉腸，佢刮你……
　　　　　打到嚟已經嘈住我瞓架喇，第二，我叫你……
　　　　　你唔醒不特止，你聽到我話「阿琪」個名仲
　　　　　即刻爆晒粗，仲醒咗我一嘢，依家俾我執番嘢
　　　　　先。（打了寬一下，寬痛）

寬：　　　頂……咪玩呢……講啦……

大：　　　第三，佢知到你醉到咁就話得喇，佢話其實
　　　　　就唔係佢想搵你……佢好似好唔妥你醉咗咁
　　　　　喎……

寬：　　　咁佢……打嚟做乜呀？

大：　　　……佢話係你阿媽刮你，打極電話都搵你唔
　　　　　倒，半夜打俾阿琪……睇吓你喉唔喉佢度，
　　　　　所以就驚動埋佢，佢咪打俾你哋嘅老死刮你囉…
　　　　　最後就喺我呢度刮倒你囉。跟住就話得喇會匯
　　　　　報返俾伯母知就收線。佢好似好唔妥你醉咗咁
　　　　　喎……

　　　　　（寬即尋找電話。）

大：　　　你同阿琪有啲嘢喎？呢排飲得咁密。

寬：　　　……個幾月無見喇……

大：　　　咩嘢料先？

KUAN	Thanks. Wow. Holy shit. (*Holds head.*)
DA	(*From inside*) Hey, Qi was looking everywhere for you…
KUAN	What? Looking for me?
DA	She called here for you. (*Da enters.*)
KUAN	Why didn't you wake me?
DA	(*Hands Kuan the towel.*) One: You asshole. She was looking for you, but she woke me up too. Two: I called you. Not only did you not get up, when you heard it was Qi, you swore your head off. And then you hit me. I want revenge now. (*Hits Kuan once. Kuan winces.*)
KUAN	Damn… Stop it. Tell me…
DA	Three: When she knew you were drunk she said to forget it. She said she wasn't really looking for you… I think she was mad at you for being drunk…
KUAN	So… why did she call me?
DA	…She said your mom was looking for you. She couldn't find you and called Qi in the middle of the night… to see if you were there. So that panicked her and she called your buddies… Finally she called here. Then she said, never mind, she'd report back to your mom. Then she hung up. She seemed pretty upset about your drinking.

(*Kuan looks for phone.*)

寬：　　　……收皮啦……

大：　　　咩嘢料呀？

寬：　　　……佢知到咗郭瑤……

大：　　　吓……嘩……你仲有同青島姐姐咩咩……

寬：　　　無呀，一早就無啦。

大：　　　咁阿琪點知？

寬：　　　話時話，係咪你講過呀？

大：　　　喂，我唔係好多架至喝……你啲嘢。況且……做男人嘅，我點會爆俾你條女知先。

寬：　　　你收皮啦你……

大：　　　唔好賴我，阿忠啩。

寬：　　　仆佢個街。唉……

大：　　　喂，你玩認真架同阿琪。

寬：　　　屌，唔撚講喇。

大：　　　OK，玩認真吓話！算數。打番俾人囉玩認真就……你唔走就我行先，你自己「彭」埋度門就得嘞。係喎，打番俾你阿媽好喎。

寬：　　　你去邊？

大：　　　返工呀。

DA	Something wrong between you and Qi? You're drinking a lot these days.
KUAN	… Haven't seen her in months…
DA	What's up?
KUAN	… Shut up…
DA	What's up?
KUAN	… She found out about Guo Yao…
DA	What? Woah… You're still with Miss Qingdao?
KUAN	No. Not for a long time.
DA	Then how did Qi find out?
KUAN	That's right. Did you tell her?
DA	Hey, I don't know a whole lot about your stuff. Besides, guys don't blab stuff to each other's girlfriends.
KUAN	Shut up…
DA	Don't blame me. Maybe it was Zhong.
KUAN	Bastard. (*Sighs.*)
DA	Hey, you getting serious with Qi?
KUAN	Fuck it. I don't want to talk about it anymore.
DA	OK. You wanna get serious, fine. Call her back… I'm gonna take off first. Shut the door when you leave. Oh yeah, and call your mom back.
KUAN	Where you going?
DA	Work.

寬：　　你返工？唔係嘛。

大：　　要老竇俾錢都要返鋪頭做啲戲嘅。

　　　　（*大口欲離開。*）

寬：　　喂，我個電話呢？

大：　　喺房，自己攞，叉爆架喇。（*開始離開。*）你都係唔好飲嘞呢排，睇住阿媽，我都想睇我阿媽，不過都唔知佢喺邊！

寬：　　得嘞。

大：　　要幫手出聲！

寬：　　OK。喂，唔該晒……

大：　　OK……打埋俾阿琪囉……

　　　　（*大口離開。*）

　　　　（*寬入房拿電話出，打電話，電話響了數下寬就收線。停了一會，再打電話。*）

寬：　　喂，媽……

　　　　（*此場完。*）

KUAN	You? Work? Are you serious?
DA	I still gotta make it look good, even if I'm just working for my old man.

(*Da Kou is about to leave.*)

KUAN	Hey. Where's my phone?
DA	In the room. Get it yourself. I recharged it. (*About to leave.*) You better lay off the booze. Look after your mom. I wish I could…if I knew where she was.
KUAN	I will.
DA	If you need anything, let me know.
KUAN	OK. Hey, thanks…
DA	OK. Call Qi…

(*Da Kou exits.*)

(*Kuan retrieves phone from bedroom, calls. Kuan hangs up after a few rings. Stops a moment and then calls again.*)

KUAN	Hello, mom?

(*End of scene.*)

第十三場 公園一角

（一個女子和寬坐在公園長椅上，女子身邊有幾個名牌時裝的購物袋，穿著時尚、名牌衣服，戴上很大的太陽眼鏡。寬的身邊有一個『阿翁鮑魚』的外賣袋。）

寬：　（寬打開手上的飯盒。）嘩！（挾起一隻雞蛋大的鮑魚又望望女子笑。）

女：　（普通話）怎麼了？

寬：　（普通話）沒甚麼！謝謝！（挾起鮑魚向女子表示謝意。）

女：　（普通話）不客氣？吃吧！（女子和寬一起笑了。）

寬：　（普通話），我不客氣，我真的餓。（寬食飯。）

　　　（一靜。）

女：　（普通話）突然找你，嚇著你了吧！

寬：　（普通話）不是你，是鮑魚！

女：　（普通話）打擾你吃飯，不好意思。

寬：　（普通話）沒有，OK呀。如果你今天晚上有空……我可以請你們食飯。

女：　（普通話）今晚就走。

寬：　（普通話）那下一次吧。

女：　（普通話）不用客氣。

SCENE 13 – IN THE CORNER OF A PARK

(*A woman sits on a park bench with Kuan. There are a few luxury brand shopping bags next to her. She is fashionably dressed in brand names and wears large sunglasses. There is a take-out bag next to Kuan that says "Grandpa's Abalone".*)

KUAN   (*Opens the rice box.*) Wow. (*Picks up a piece of abalone as big as an egg with his chopsticks, looks at the woman and smiles.*)

WOMAN   (*In Putonghua*) What's wrong?

KUAN   (*In Putonghua*) Nothing. Thank you. (*Picks up the abalone and expresses thanks to the woman.*)

WOMAN   (*In Putonghua*) You're welcome. Eat! (*She laughs with Kuan.*)

KUAN   (*In Putonghua*) I am really hungry. I won't wait then. (*Eats.*)

     (*Silence.*)

WOMAN   (*In Putonghua*) This sudden visit scared you?

KUAN   (*In Putonghua*) I got scared by the abalone, not you.

WOMAN   (*In Putonghua*) Sorry to bother you at lunch.

KUAN   (*In Putonghua*) No problem. It's OK. If you're OK tonight… let me take you guys out for dinner.

WOMAN   (*In Putonghua*) We're leaving tonight.

KUAN   (*In Putonghua*) Next time then.

WOMAN   (*In Putonghua*) You're too kind.

寬：　　　（*普通話*）不是客氣……應該的……

女：　　　（*突然大聲*）（*普通話*）你跟我就別來這一套
　　　　　啦。

寬：　　　（*普通話*）……好……

女：　　　（*即笑*）（*普通話*）好，下次你請。

　　　　　（*靜，寬繼續食飯。*）

女：　　　（*普通話*）其實我經常來香港。

寬：　　　唔唔。

　　　　　（*一頓。*）

女：　　　（*普通話*）你好嗎？

寬：　　　（*普通話*）還好，看來你比我好。

女：　　　（*普通話*）我……還好。

寬：　　　（*普通話*）那就好啦。

女：　　　（*普通話*）我現在確實挺好的。

寬：　　　Good。

女：　　　（*普通話*）他對我挺好，每次來都帶著我。

寬：　　　（*普通話*）你們住在青島！

女：　　　（*普通話*）現在搬到上海去了。其實我們都喜
　　　　　歡青島，我們的爸媽又都在那兒。但是沒辦
　　　　　法，生意全在上海！

KUAN   (*In Putonghua*) It's not kindness. I really should...

WOMAN   (*In Putonghua, suddenly loudly*) Stop this act with me.

KUAN   (*In Putonghua*) ... OK...

WOMAN   (*Laughs. In Putonghua*) All right. Your treat next time.

              (*Silence. Kuan continues to eat.*)

WOMAN   (*In Putonghua*) Actually, I come to Hong Kong often.

KUAN   Uh huh.

              (*A moment.*)

WOMAN   (*In Putonghua*) How are you?

KUAN   (*In Putonghua*) I'm fine. Probably not as good as you.

WOMAN   (*In Putonghua*) I'm... all right.

KUAN   (*In Putonghua*) That's good.

WOMAN   (*In Putonghua*) I really am good now.

KUAN   Good.

WOMAN   (*In Putonghua*) He's very good to me. Every time he comes here, he brings me.

KUAN   (*In Putonghua*) You both live in Qingdao?

WOMAN   (*In Putonghua*) We're living in Shanghai now. Actually, we like Qingdao. Our parents are there. But the business is in Shanghai. What can you do?

寬：　　（*普通話*）他一定是很忙，沒時間陪你？所以你自己去shopping。

女：　　（*普通話*）我們每天都在一起。公司的活兒我們都一起幹，以前給別人當秘書，現在乾脆給他當秘書了。哈……不過現在主要的工作就是吃飯。

寬：　　（*普通話*）做生意就是這樣的。

女：　　（*普通話*）……唉……做生意就是做關係，每天晚上就是飯局，沒完沒了的喝酒，你不喝到吐人家就不會放過你。尤其是做地產的，全都是跟那些當官兒的打交道。有時候酒還沒有醒，又要去跟別人再喝。我經常跟他一起去，他也喜歡，我也可以照顧照顧他。

寬：　　（*普通話*）那挺好呀……對……去年你結婚的時候還沒有恭喜你。

女：　　（*突然望寬又轉開，輕鬆地*）（*普通話*）有呀……你在電話裡說了！

寬：　　……唔……

　　　　　（*靜。*）

女：　　（*普通話*）你……你現在跟女朋友好嗎？

寬：　　（*普通話*）好。

女：　　（*普通話*）那就好。

寬：　　（*普通話*）……不好……

KUAN   (*In Putonghua*) He must be too busy to spend time with you. You're shopping alone.

WOMAN   (*In Putonghua*) We're together every day. We do everything together for the business. I used to be someone else's secretary. Now I'm his secretary. Ha... But my main task now is eating.

KUAN   (*In Putonghua*) That's part of the business?

WOMAN   (*Sighs. In Putonghua*) Business is all about connections. Dinner every night and endless drinking. They won't let up until you puke. Especially the real estate business. It's all about making connections with people in the government. Sometimes, before you sober up from one meal, you're off drinking with someone else. I always go out with him. He likes that. I can take care of him.

KUAN   (*In Putonghua*) That's great... Oh yeah... I never congratulated you on your wedding last year.

WOMAN   (*Suddenly looks at Kuan, then turns away. Casually, in Putonghua*) You did... you said it on the phone.

KUAN   Mmm...

        (*Silence.*)

WOMAN   (*In Putonghua*) How... how are things with your girlfriend?

KUAN   (*In Putonghua*) Good.

WOMAN   (*In Putonghua*) That's good.

KUAN   (*In Putonghua*) ...Not good...

女：　　　啊。

寬：　　　（*普通話*）對，不好。

女：　　　（*故意取笑寬*）（*普通話*）一定是你「不好」……所以不好啦。

　　　　　（*女子又笑，寬跟著笑。*）

女：　　　（*普通話*）我們像嗎？

寬：　　　（*普通話*）一點點……比你年青……當空姐的……

女：　　　（*普通話*）空姐……原來你喜歡了一個空姐。

寬：　　　（*普通話*）不是，認識的時候不是。不過是在飛機上認識的，同一班飛機回香港……坐在一起。她家在加拿大。

女：　　　（*普通話*）我去深圳是為了工作。可她為甚麼，加拿大不是很好嗎？

寬：　　　（*普通話*）怕悶，喜歡香港好玩。

女：　　　（*普通話*）年輕都喜歡玩，你們一定很合得來。

寬：　　　（*普通話*）你不用兜個圈來說我只懂玩！……（*停*）現在……我們不是很好……不說！

WOMAN   Oh!

KUAN   (*In Putonghua*) Yeah, not good.

WOMAN   (*Purposely teasing him, in Putonghua*) It must be you who is "not good"… That's why it's not good.

(*She laughs. Then he laughs.*)

WOMAN   (*In Putonghua*) Do we look alike?

KUAN   (*In Putonghua*) Huh? A little… But she's younger… She's a flight attendant…

WOMAN   (*In Putonghua*) Flight attendant… So you fancy a flight attendant.

KUAN   (*In Putonghua*) No, she didn't used to be one. But we met on the plane. We flew on the same flight to Hong Kong… we sat together. Her home is in Canada.

WOMAN   (*In Putonghua*) I went to Shenzhen for work. Why does she do it? Canada is nice, right?

KUAN   (*In Putonghua*) She finds it boring there. She says Hong Kong is more fun.

WOMAN   (*In Putonghua*) Young people always want fun. You must get along very well.

KUAN   (*In Putonghua*) You don't have to find an excuse to say that I only want to have fun! (*Stops.*) In any case, we're not getting along now… Let's talk about something else.

女： （*普通話*）你就是這樣，説一半又不説了。我有話就要説清楚，不像你。（*一頓*）你不喜歡我我就走開，我不要不明不白。

（*寬靜了下來。*）

女： （*普通話*）對不起。不説了。

寬： （*普通話*）對不起。

女： OK。

寬： （*普通話*）我説「對不起」。

女： 唔……

寬： （*普通話*）我跟她在一起……所以不找你。

女： （*普通話*）……是你不讓我找到你。

寬： （*普通話*）對。

女： （*普通話*）其實我沒有想過再找你。

（*停頓。*）

寬： （*普通話*）對不起，上一次跟到青島去……香港人不是這樣想，你爸媽都是好人，我以為他們都明白……我沒想過那麼早結婚……我以為大家都明白……（*廣東話*）我唔係話「我同你淨係玩吓」，我地一齊真係開心……其實你……

WOMAN   (*In Putonghua*) You never change. You never finish what you want to say. Unlike you, I always say what's on my mind. (*A moment.*) You didn't want me so I got out of the way. I don't want any misunderstanding.

(*Kuan quiets down.*)

WOMAN   (*In Putonghua*) Sorry. Let's change the subject.

KUAN   (*In Putonghua*) I'm sorry.

WOMAN   OK.

KUAN   (*In Putonghua*) I said, I'm sorry.

WOMAN   Mm...

KUAN   (*In Putonghua*) I broke it off with you... because I met her.

WOMAN   (*In Putonghua*) You wouldn't let me contact you anymore.

KUAN   (*In Putonghua*) Yes.

WOMAN   (*In Putonghua*) Actually, I wasn't going to contact you.

(*Pause.*)

KUAN   (*In Putonghua*) I'm sorry. I just thought that since we both had time off, we'd vacation in Qingdao... Hong Kong people don't think like that. Your parents were great. I thought they understood... I never thought about getting married so early... I thought we understood each other... (*In Cantonese*) I didn't mean that "I just wanted to fool around with you". We had a good time... Actually, you...

女： （*普通話*）「其實」都過去了。

（*一頓。*）

女： （*普通話*）我以為兩個人在一起開心……很自然就會走在一起。可能你還在享受你的浪漫，我到南方來找的也是浪漫，但是我不覺得結了婚就沒有呀。只要找到一個深愛的人，能夠一起生活，一起吃飯，生孩子，不用天天吃鮑魚燕窩也可以過得很快樂。知道自己想要的是甚麼就夠了，做人就是這麼簡單。以前你總是說你要做甚麼一流的設計師，有一天會用我的名字來做你的品牌……多開心啊……或者是你喝得太多了吧。

（*一頓。*）

女： （*普通話*）可這些都不是我的追求。（*突然笑笑指著身邊的購物袋*）這就是命吧，你看這些東西我現在多的是！

（*一頓。*）

女： （*突然有點失控*）（*普通話*）如果你是愛了別人我沒話可說，但是你就這樣跑了……

寬： （*看著女子*）（*普通話*）郭瑤……

女： （*看著寬，開懷地笑著地*）……（*普通話*）我們是兩個世界的人，對嗎！？大陸人、香港人！

（*很長的靜。*）

WOMAN (*In Putonghua*) "Actually", it's all over.

(*A moment.*)

WOMAN (*In Putonghua*) I thought that when two people are happy together… it's natural they would want to be together. Maybe you were still enjoying the romance. I came to the south to find romance, but I didn't think that romance would end when I got married. As long as you find someone you love, you can live together, eat together, have children. You can be happy without abalone and swallow's nest every day. Knowing what you want is enough. Life is that simple. You used to say you wanted to be a first class designer. One day, you'd use my name as a brand name… Happy times… Maybe you'd had too much to drink.

(*A moment.*)

WOMAN (*In Putonghua*) But that wasn't what I wanted. (*Laughs suddenly at the bags beside her.*) That's fate. Look at what I have in my life now.

(*A moment.*)

WOMAN (*Suddenly a little out of control, in Putonghua*) If you fell in love with someone else, there was nothing I could do. But you ran…

KUAN (*Looks at her. In Cantonese*) Guo Yao…

WOMAN (*Looks at Kuan. Laughs heartily. In Putonghua*) We belong to different worlds, don't we? China and Hong Kong.

(*Long silence.*)

女： （*普通話*）我懷孕了。

寬： （*普通話*）是嗎？是男還是女？

女： （*普通話*）都喜歡。他說「女兒」更好，貼心小棉襖，不怕沒人要。

寬： （*普通話*）你們只准生一個架嗎！

女： （*普通話*）到香港來生嘛。只有一個孩子！將來我們老了，他會很孤獨的。

寬： （*普通話*）想得真遠！

（*靜。*）

女： （*普通話*）你快跟女朋友結婚，（*廣東話*）生個仔。（*普通話*）那你爸媽多開心哪。

寬： （*廣東話*）我呢份人自己都未掂，仲生仔？

女： （*廣東話*）係呀，「份人」係無得改架。你真係唔係幾好架。

（*兩人笑。*）

（*女子電話響，接電話。*）

女： （*普通話*）喂，買到啦，好多人呀，好像全國人民都到LV來了。我現在過來。好吧。我沒事，很好。（*摸摸自己的肚*）你兒子當然沒事了，我怎麼會餓著他呢？！神經病！好啦好啦……（*收線*）（*廣東話*）我夠鐘搵我老公，你仲未食完喎。

WOMAN (*In Putonghua*) I'm pregnant.

KUAN (*In Putonghua*) Really? Boy or girl?

WOMAN (*In Putonghua*) We like both. He said a girl is better. Daddy's girl. Someone will want her.

KUAN (*In Putonghua*) You can only have one child?

WOMAN (*In Putonghua*) We can have more in Hong Kong. With one child, when we get old, it will be tough for him.

KUAN (*In Putonghua*) That's thinking ahead.

(*Silence.*)

WOMAN (*In Putonghua*) Marry your girlfriend. (*In Cantonese*) Have a baby. (*In Putonghua*) Make your parents happy.

KUAN (*In Cantonese*) Have a baby? I'm a mess.

WOMAN (*In Cantonese*) Yes. "You" can't change. You're really not that good of a catch.

(*They laugh.*)

(*Woman's phone rings. She answers.*)

WOMAN (*In Putonghua*) Hello? I bought it. It was crowded, like the whole world was at LV. I'll come over now. OK. I'm fine. Good. (*Touches her tummy.*) Of course your son is fine. Why would I starve him?! You're crazy. OK, OK… (*Hangs up. In Cantonese*) I have to meet my husband. You haven't finished your lunch.

寬： 　（*廣東話*）得啦。我會食，好嘢我唔嘥。

　　　（*女子望著寬突然笑出來，女子再望著前方。一頓。*）

女： 　（*普通話*）哎……我告訴你，我不會再找你的。

寬： 　（*普通話*）明白。

女： 　（*廣東話*）我唔會同你做朋友架。

　　　（*女子開始起身。*）

寬： 　（*普通話*）郭瑤，謝謝。

　　　（*女子不語，開始離開。*）

寬： 　（*普通話*）再見。

　　　（*女子停一停，沒有回頭，離開。*）

　　　（*寬打電話，出現是阿琪的電話錄音。*）

琪： 　（*VO*）Hi, I'm in another part of the world. Don't be sad. Please leave your message. I'll call you back soon. Bye!

　　　（*長的「啤」聲。*）

　　　（*此場完。*）

KUAN   (*In Cantonese*) It's fine. I'll finish. I wouldn't waste the good stuff.

(*Woman looks at Kuan and suddenly laughs. She looks ahead. A moment.*)

WOMAN   (*In Putonghua*) Oh, listen. I won't contact you anymore.

KUAN   OK.

WOMAN   (*In Cantonese*) I won't be your friend.

(*She rises.*)

KUAN   (*In Putonghua*) Guo Yao. Thank you.

(*She doesn't speak. She starts to leave.*)

KUAN   (*In Putonghua*) Goodbye.

(*She stops but does not look back. Leaves.*)

(*Kuan dials his phone. We hear Qi's voice mail message.*)

QI   (*VO*) Hi, I'm in another part of the world. Don't be sad. Please leave your message. I'll call you back soon. Bye!

(*Long beep.*)

(*End of scene.*)

第十四場：寬媽家中

（寬的家姐拿著一個健康枕頭，準備放入一個大膠袋。）

姐： 佢話呢個先瞓得舒服。陣，咪一樣，我都特登買咗個新俾佢，係都要呢個！

（寬把一個旅行箱從房推出來。）

寬： 應該夠喇啩，唔夠先再攞啦。

姐： 夏天衫都攞埋去？駛唔駛呀。

寬： 好快就熱架喇。攞埋先囉。

姐： 邊有咁多地方呀我嗰度。

寬： 咁你攞番出嚟喇。

姐： 唏，執咗就算啦。費事又要執過。

寬： 玩咩，神又係你，鬼又係你。執唔執呀？

姐： 唔執喇，講吓都唔得呀！咁躁做乜啫你？

寬： 你躁定我躁呀！

姐： 你躁囉！Call定的士先。

寬： 落去截咪得囉，駛乜call呀！

姐： 平廿幾蚊架，做乜唔call！

寬： 我俾囉。

SCENE 14 – KUAN'S MOTHER'S HOME

(Kuan's sister is putting a health pillow into a large plastic bag.)

SISTER She said this one is more comfortable. It's the usual thing. I bought her a new pillow but she still wants this one.

(Kuan brings out a suitcase from the room.)

KUAN I think this is enough. I'll get another one if it's not.

SISTER You're taking summer clothes? I don't think we'll need them.

KUAN The weather will warm up soon. Let's just take it.

SISTER I don't have that much room.

KUAN Then leave it.

SISTER It's already packed. I don't want us to have to pack it again.

KUAN So do you want to take it or not?

SISTER No. What's the matter with you? I can't even talk about it?

KUAN Not me! What's the matter with you!

SISTER It's you! Call a cab.

KUAN What for? We can get one downstairs.

SISTER You get $20 off. Why don't you call?

KUAN I'll pay for it.

姐：　　　邊個俾都係架啦，有得平點解唔call啫。

寬：　　　好煩呀。唔call。

姐：　　　是但你，唔好咁燥唔該。有冇嘢飲，好頸渴。

寬：　　　自己去雪櫃睇吓。

　　　　　（姐入廚房。）

姐：　　　（從內）你要唔要呀？

寬：　　　是但吖。

　　　　　（姐出來。）

姐：　　　有清涼茶同綠茶，要邊隻你？

寬：　　　是但！

姐：　　　唔好是但，你飲清涼茶嘞，你咁燥。

　　　　　（把清涼茶遞給寬，自己飲綠茶，寬也飲，寬
　　　　　拿出銀包掏錢。）

寬：　　　俾住八千蚊你先。夠唔夠？

姐：　　　得啦，上次照片嗰次萬幾都未俾番你。

寬：　　　由佢囉。

姐：　　　唔好，呀媽大家都有份。下個月你唔駛俾我住
　　　　　啦。再下個月先啦。

寬：　　　都話我請個工人咯。

SISTER	It's a discount no matter who pays. Why don't you call?
KUAN	You're driving me crazy. I'm not calling.
SISTER	Suit yourself. And calm down. Is there anything to drink? I'm thirsty.
KUAN	Go and look in the fridge yourself.
	(*Sister goes to kitchen.*)
SISTER	(*From inside*) Do you want anything?
KUAN	Whatever.
	(*Sister enters.*)
SISTER	There's herbal tea and green tea. Which one do you want?
KUAN	Whichever.
SISTER	Don't "whichever" me. You take the herbal tea. Cool your temper.
	(*Hands Kuan the herbal tea. She drinks the green tea. Kuan drinks, and takes out money from his wallet.*)
KUAN	I'll give you $8,000 first. Is that enough?
SISTER	Yeah. I haven't paid you back the $10,000 for the scan.
KUAN	Don't worry about it.
SISTER	No, she's our mother. You don't have to pay me for living expenses. Just wait until next month.
KUAN	I said I'll hire a maid.

姐： 　等你請倒返嚟蚊都瞓啦。姐夫佢無嘢嘅，個工人過咗嚟個女又邊個煮俾佢食吖？

寬： 　你唔識你阿媽呀。佢淨係覺得屋企最好架。

姐： 　依家到你中唔中意咩。你放工上嚟食飯佢咪中意囉，佢最擔心你無湯飲啫。

寬： 　得啦。

姐： 　叫埋阿琪上嚟囉。

寬： 　得啦……

姐： 　係喎，佢尋日嚟探過阿媽喎，仲買咗兩盒冬蟲草嚟添。做乜會淨係佢自己上嚟唔同你一齊呀。

寬： 　佢上去咩尋日？

姐： 　你唔知！

寬： 　……佢返咗加拿大成個月……

姐： 　返咗嚟都唔知！你哋有啲嘢喎。

寬： 　有乜嘢啫……

姐： 　唧係有嘢囉。

　　　（*兩人飲手上的飲品。*）

姐： 　佢就有「答覆」過你嘞，都幾識做人，睇嚟都唔係玩玩吓，OK嘅。

SISTER	By the time you hire someone, she would already be on her third treatment. Your brother-in-law is fine. The maid is at your house. Who's going to cook for our daughter?
KUAN	Don't you know your own mother? She likes it best at home.
SISTER	You don't have a choice now. She'll like it as long as you come to dinner after work. All she worries about is your not drinking enough soup.
KUAN	Fine.
SISTER	Get Qi to come too.
KUAN	I know…
SISTER	Oh yeah, she came to visit mom yesterday and brought two boxes of cordiceps. Why didn't you come with her?
KUAN	She went up yesterday?
SISTER	Didn't you know?
KUAN	…She was in Canada for a whole month…
SISTER	She's back, don't you know? Is something wrong between you two?
KUAN	Nothing…
SISTER	That means yes.
	(*They drink.*)
SISTER	She's more responsible than you. And she's clever. I don't think she plays around. She's all right.

寬： 兩盒冬蟲草就同佢講咁多好說話。

姐： 你當我係咩。人哋一個女仔喺度，你都唔好好咁對人，你仲話我。

寬： 喂，我點唔好呀，佢講咩呀！

姐： 我乜都唔知！我唔喺度！你哋依家玩晒嘢佢都嚟喎。你自己好自為之啦。

寬： 嘩，你真係當我好衰咁喎。

姐： 你自己至知嘞真係。你唔細架喇，你無諗住結婚架咩。仲未玩夠呀？

寬： 要結嗰陣咪結囉，無厘頭結咩婚啫。

姐： 阿媽唔知會點，如果電完唔得，我真係唔敢諗，不過如果你結埋婚佢都會安樂啲嘅我諗。

寬： 邊度搵個人嚟結呀，係咪落街是但搵個女人……「我驚呀媽唔擺得幾耐，你幫幫手沖喜吓吖唔該」。係咪咁呀。

姐： 哼，你做乜啫，駛唔駛咁惡呀。唔講嘞，OK。OK。

寬： 你估結婚玩架。

KUAN   Two boxes of cordiceps and she's a saint.

SISTER   Don't you go on about me. She's a good girl. You should treat her properly.

KUAN   How did I mistreat her? What did she say?

SISTER   I don't know anything. I'm not here. She's still coming around after everything you did. You better think about it.

KUAN   Geez, you think I'm that bad?!

SISTER   Only you know that. You're not young anymore. Have you thought about getting married? Haven't you had enough fun?

KUAN   You don't just get married out of the blue. I'll get married when I'm ready.

SISTER   I don't know how mom is going to handle it. If the chemo doesn't work, I don't dare think about what might happen. But if you got married, I think she might feel content.

KUAN   Where am I gonna find someone? Just grab someone off the street? "Excuse me, I'm afraid my mom won't survive long. Could you marry me to make a happy occasion?" Something like that?

SISTER   Christ, you don't have to bite my head off. What's the matter with you? Fine, forget it. OK?

KUAN   You think marriage is a game?

姐：　　　OK，講完喇。走。我call的士。開門，你攞個
　　　　　喼。

　　　　　（*姐開門出邊打電話，寬提起旅行喼跟著，離
　　　　　開邊行邊大聲講。*）

寬：　　　不如你生多個嚟沖吓吖。

　　　　　（*此場完。*）

SISTER   OK. Forget it. Let's go. I'll call a cab. Open the door. Take the suitcase.

          (*Sister opens the door and calls. Kuan takes the suitcase and follows.*)

KUAN   (*As he exists, loudly*) Why don't you have another baby to make a happy occasion?

          (*End of scene.*)

第十五場：流行咖啡室

（*媽坐在椅上一人，不知所措四處望。*）

（*寬手上拿著一杯咖啡和一樽奇異果汁入。*）

寬： 媽！奇異果汁，無唔凍架。

媽： 是但啦，我都唔係好頸渴。

（*寬坐下。*）

媽： 你飲咖啡！唔好成日飲咁多咖啡呀。你成日飲架？

寬： 間唔中。

媽： ……開唔到，你幫我扭。

（*寬幫她開。*）

媽： 嘩，好凍。（*放下不喝。*）

寬： 去買過第二啲嘢俾你飲。

媽： 唔駛，攤一陣。

寬： 坐一陣走。未夠鐘，而家至兩點半。

（*稍停。*）

媽： （*拿銀包*）我俾定錢你一陣睇醫生，要成三千幾蚊架呢個醫生。

寬： 得啦，我有。介紹你嗰個又係做緊電療呀？

SCENE 15 – A POPULAR COFFEE HOUSE

(*Mother sits in a chair by herself. She looks around uncomfortably.*)

(*Kuan enters with a cup of coffee and a glass of kiwi juice.*)

KUAN   Mom, kiwi juice. They don't have anything warm.

MOTHER   Whatever. I'm not thirsty.

(*Kuan sits.*)

MOTHER   You having coffee? Don't drink so much coffee. Do you drink it all day?

KUAN   Once in a while.

MOTHER   …I can't open it. Twist it open for me.

(*Kuan helps her.*)

MOTHER   Wow, it's cold. (*Puts down drink.*)

KUAN   I'll buy you something else.

MOTHER   Forget it. Just leave it to warm.

KUAN   Let's sit for a while. It's early yet. Only 2:30.

(*Pause.*)

MOTHER   (*Takes out wallet.*) I'll give you some money now for the doctor. This doctor costs over $3,000.

KUAN   It's fine. I got it. The person who recommended him is also in chemo?

媽：　　前日去劃線嗰陣一齊等講開，佢話佢都睇緊。係西醫不過都用中藥。好多人都睇。

寬：　　好多人都會中西一齊用。

（*靜。*）

媽：　　成日飲咖啡，湯你又唔飲。

寬：　　得啦！

媽：　　你家姐又係，叫佢飲淡湯好似叫佢飲毒藥咁，兩個都係咁，揀飲擇食。

寬：　　煩得過佢！食碗雲吞麵都逐粒蔥揀出嚟。

媽：　　你老竇就好呢，煮乜就食乜。

寬：　　咁魚生你夠唔食啦。芝士你都唔食。

媽：　　佢係食煙衰，一瞓醒就點支煙！

（*靜。*）

媽：　　顧家嗰度好。一個月三十日就做三十日。人蠢囉，擔屎都唔偷食！

寬：　　邊個擔屎會偷食架！

媽：　　窮嗰下弊呢。唔係共產黨嚟？我真係唔會嫁俾你老竇。啲人仲話我犀利喇嫁個香港人！

MOTHER   We were in the waiting room and started talking about it. He said he is seeing this doctor. A western doctor who uses Chinese medicine. He has lots of patients.

KUAN   A lot of people go to both Chinese and western doctors.

(*Silence.*)

MOTHER   You'll drink coffee all day, but not soup.

KUAN   I know.

MOTHER   Your sister is the same. You'd think I had asked her to drink poison when I give her soup. You are both the same. Picky eaters.

KUAN   She's worse! She picks all the green onions out of every wonton in her noodles.

MOTHER   Your father was great. He ate everything I cooked.

KUAN   You won't eat sushi either, or cheese.

MOTHER   His only vice was smoking. He lit up as soon as he woke up.

(*Silence.*)

MOTHER   And he took care of us. He worked every day of the week. What a fool. Never cheated a day in his life.

KUAN   You wouldn't have married a cheater.

MOTHER   But he was poor. If it weren't because the communists were coming, I would never have married your dad. Everyone thought I did well, marrying a Hong Kong man.

寬： 我哋有錢定你哋屋企有錢啲？

媽： 你哋耕田養豬有咩錢呀！你老竇好細就出咗嚟學師！返去娶我之嘛。

（*靜*。）

媽： 你哋條村真係好窮架以前，你阿爺留俾你老竇間屋好巴閉架喇算。

寬： 巴咩閉呀？圍住果啲而家間間都四五層高！

媽： 而家個個都起過晒啦，係淨番你哋間。呀大眼叔早幾年都起啦，佢哋仲窮過你老竇呀以前。我講你聽初初嫁番你哋度真係陰功，又未有你哋，成日一個人同四面牆。你阿嫲又盲啦，你老豆又淨係過節至返吓嚟，唉！我嫁到嚟都唔知幾悶。咁呀大眼叔同你老竇同村兄弟吖嗎，有時分到嘅乜就俾啲我，又過我哋屋度坐天井傾偈啦，你話啲人幾衰呀就話我哋好喝，你老豆又淨係過節至返吓嚟，啲人就講我哋。唉！我嫁到嚟都唔知幾悶。

寬： 咁你可以返吓去婆婆度架嗎，好近啫。

KUAN   Who had more money, your family or dad's family?

MOTHER   Your dad's family were farmers. They were poor. Your father started working away from home very young. When he returned home, he married me.

(*Silence.*)

MOTHER   Your father's village was very poor. The house that your grandfather left your father was considered not too shabby.

KUAN   Not too shabby? Everything around it now is four or five stories high.

MOTHER   Everyone has rebuilt taller houses now. Your father's house is the only one left. Uncle Big Eye rebuilt it a few years ago. They were even poorer than your father. When I first married into your father's family, it was horrible. You weren't born yet. I sat in the house alone all the time. Your grandmother was blind. Your father only returned home during the holidays. (*Sighs.*) I was so lonely after my wedding. So Uncle Big Eye, your father's buddy from the village, would give me whatever he managed to get his hands on. Sometimes he came over to chat with me. Then someone spread rumors about us. Your father only came home during the holidays, so people started talking about us. (*Sighs.*) I was so bored after I got married.

KUAN   You could have gone home to visit your mother. She was close by.

媽： 以前無話成日返外家架！以前……細個我屋企好多人架。我最細啦，你婆婆有嘢食就叫晒全部人去晒佢間屋逐個派，嗱，我五個大佬除咗你三舅父早唔喺度，一人四個仔兩個女，係四舅父就三個女，成日都成班細路喺條巷度走嚟走去，唔係去你婆婆間屋，就去你三舅母度，你婆婆有嘢食就叫晒全部人去晒佢間屋逐個派，幾開心架！係後尾我個五哥要掙埋婆婆間屋至搞到唔眹之嘛，連佢啲仔女都都衰埋一份。連阿嫲都唔叫聲，過年都無話去拜個年，係我啲嫂衰教啲仔囡講事講非，走去鬧你婆婆，『死老鬼，偏心鬼』咁樣鬧佢阿嫲。咁嘅人都有架喎！不過佢哋細，我出咗嚟佢哋至出世，你無見過囉！

寬： 你哋有錢過我老豆好多架。

媽： 我阿媽嫁入嚟都有個妹仔陪嫁架，後尾落咗嚟香港我都有去探過佢。土改嗰陣咪俾人鬧我哋屋企係地主囉。『死地主仔』咁鬧我架！最辛苦嗰啲呢……啲人就叫你去做，功分你就得最小。有個村頭嗰家嘅真係好衰，嗰陣去起水庫勞動……我細個嗰陣真係邊駛做架啫，真係無估到……幾條村一齊去起水庫，我呢真係擔唔

MOTHER   You couldn't just leave whenever you wanted to back then. When I was little, there were lots of people in my home. I was the youngest. Whenever there was something to eat, your grandmother would tell everyone to come and share. My five brothers, except for your third uncle who died early, each had four sons and two daughters. Your fourth uncle had three daughters. There were always kids running in and out of the alleys. Either they went to your grandmother's house or they went to third auntie's house. Every time your grandmother had food, she would call everyone to her house to get some. So much fun. My five brothers only stopped talking to each other when they started fighting over our mother's house. Even their children turned evil. Our mother never said a word. They never came by during Chinese New Year. My sisters-in-law were so hateful. They corrupted their kids, and got them to scold your grandmother. "Bloody old fool playing favorites." That's what they said to your grandmother. How could they do that?! But they were young. They were born after I left. You never met them.

KUAN   Your family was that much richer than dad's?

MOTHER   When my mother married, her servant girl accompanied her. After I came to Hong Kong, I still went back to visit them. During the land reform, our family was blamed for being landlords. "Damn landlords." That's what they used to call us. They always made us do the worst kinds of jobs. They rewarded us the fewest labor points. The village heads were the worst. They told us to build a reservoir... I had never worked a day in my life. I never

起嗰兩兜泥，就偷偷倒咁啲啦。嗰個村頭嗰個
真係衰，見我倒咁啲佢仲「筆」返多啲落嚟。
唉，真係辛苦到我死架啦，夜晚瞓喺棚度我真
係喊一大場都瞓唔到，嗰對腳同個膊頭真係痛
到。哈，而家村頭嗰個都唔知幾巴閉，仲擺六
十幾圍呀娶新抱個陣！

（媽靜了下。）

媽： 咁就幾十年囉。

（寬望著媽。）

媽： 醫倒就醫囉。

（靜。）

寬： 媽……

媽： ……

寬： 無嘢。

媽： 你呀……就係咁，把口撬都唔開嘅。你家姐
就講到唔停，煩到你頭都痛。有嘢你就講出
嚟……你同你老竇一擔擔。佢阿媽死嗰陣佢都
無喊出過一聲。想佢呵下你都幾難，幾十年都
無話問過你一句你點點點……咁呀……

寬： （突然地）老竇佢……

媽： （好像沒有聽到寬說話）成世人出街都無話拖
下我架……

imagined… Several villages came together to build the reservoir. I couldn't carry two buckets of mud for the life of me, so I poured some out of my buckets. The village head was horrible. When he saw me pour some out of my buckets, he dumped even more back in. (*Sighs.*) It was backbreaking work. When I went to bed at night, I screamed with pain. My feet and shoulders hurt so badly. Ha…The village heads were sure hot stuff. They would have 60-odd tables for their sons' wedding banquets.

(*Mother is quiet.*)

MOTHER   That was decades ago.

(*Kuan looks at Mother.*)

MOTHER   If the treatment works, I'll take it.

(*Silence.*)

KUAN   Mom…

MOTHER   …

KUAN   Nothing.

MOTHER   You… Same old problem. You never talk. And your sister talks nonstop. She is so annoying. If you have something on your mind, speak… You're just like your dad. He never cried when his mother died. He never comforted you. Never asked how you were in all those years.

KUAN   (*Suddenly*) Dad, he…

MOTHER   (*As if she didn't hear Kuan speak*) Never held my hand when we went out…

寬： ⋯⋯我好掛住佢！

媽： ⋯⋯（*停了下來望寬，突然哭出來*）

（*媽自己在手袋中拿出紙巾。*）

媽： 佢就係成世做⋯⋯十零歲就自己出嚟學師搵食，好陰公架⋯⋯無人錫佢，佢又邊識錫人吖⋯⋯

（*長的靜默。*）

寬： 走喇。

媽： ⋯⋯夠鐘喇！

寬： 我想去買啲嘢。

媽： 買咩？

寬： （*起身*）去買部DV cam。

（*此場完。*）

KUAN   …I miss dad!

MOTHER   … (*Stops to look at Kuan. Suddenly cries.*)

            (*Mother takes out tissues from her purse.*)

MOTHER   He worked his whole life… Left home in his
            teens to learn his trade and make a living.
            What a hard life… No one loved him. How
            could he know how to love others…

            (*Long silence.*)

KUAN   Let's go.

MOTHER   … Is it time?

KUAN   I want to buy something.

MOTHER   Buy what?

KUAN   (*Rises.*) A DV camera.

            (*End of scene.*)

第十六場：琪家的樓下

（*深夜時份，寬一個人。琪慢慢拖著行李入場，停下來望著不察覺她的寬。寬回頭發現琪，兩人凝住了，靜了一會。*）

寬：　　Delay咗呀？

（*琪點頭。*）

寬：　　我打電話問過，無諗住會delay咁多。

（*琪不語，琪在手袋拿出門匙。*）

寬：　　我八點等到依家⋯⋯

（*琪不望寬。*）

寬：　　我知你返咗嚟，不過打俾你嗰陣你又飛咗。

（*琪仍是不望寬。*）

寬：　　你電話又唔開，所以⋯⋯

琪：　　（*截寬的說話*）有電話唔一定要聽架。

寬：　　係⋯⋯所以搵唔倒你！

（*靜。*）

（*琪開始離開。*）

寬：　　琪⋯⋯

（*琪停。*）

SCENE 16 – OUTSIDE OF QI'S RESIDENCE

(*It's the middle of the night. Kuan is alone. Qi enters slowly with luggage. She stops to look at Kuan, who is not aware of her. Kuan turns around and sees Qi. They stare at each other. Silence.*)

KUAN   You were delayed?

(*Qi nods.*)

KUAN   I called to ask. I didn't think you'd be delayed so long.

(*Qi doesn't speak. She takes out keys from her purse.*)

KUAN   I've been waiting since eight o'clock…

(*Qi doesn't look at Kuan.*)

KUAN   I knew you came back. But when I called you, you'd flown again.

(*Qi still doesn't look at Kuan.*)

KUAN   Your phone was off, so…

QI   (*Interrupts Kuan.*) I don't have to answer my phone.

KUAN   Yes… that's why I couldn't reach you.

(*Silence.*)

(*Qi starts to walk away.*)

KUAN   Qi…

(*Qi stops.*)

寬： 　　……你肚唔肚餓……不如……

琪： 　　（突然望寬）依家幾點？

寬： 　　（看錶）十一點兩個字……

琪： 　　你等到依家就係想知我肚唔肚餓！

寬： 　　……唔係……

琪： 　　你自己去食，唔好餓親自己。

　　　　（琪起步離開。寬搶過琪的行李箱。）

寬： 　　等陣好唔好……

　　　　（琪停下來望著行李箱不動。）

寬： 　　你聽我講……

琪： 　　我無聽咩，係你無講之嘛。

寬： 　　OK……

琪： 　　咩OK，OK咩……

寬： 　　唔係……唔OK……

琪： 　　OK。

　　　　（靜。）

寬： 　　多謝你探我阿媽。

琪： 　　唔駛客氣。

　　　　（一頓。）

琪： 　　咁無嘢啦……

寬： 　　佢叫郭瑤……

KUAN	…Are you hungry?… Why don't I…
QI	(*Suddenly looks at Kuan.*) What time is it?
KUAN	(*Looks at watch.*) Ten past eleven…
QI	That's all you want to know from me after waiting all this time?
KUAN	…No…
QI	You go ahead and eat. Don't starve yourself.
	(*Qi walks away. Kuan takes Qi's suitcase.*)
KUAN	Please wait…
	(*Qi stops and looks at suitcase.*)
KUAN	Listen to me…
QI	Haven't I been listening? You just haven't said anything.
KUAN	OK…
QI	What is OK? OK what?
KUAN	No… not OK.
QI	OK.
	(*Silence.*)
KUAN	Thanks for visiting my mom.
QI	You're welcome.
	(*A moment.*)
QI	Is that all?
KUAN	Her name is Guo Yao.

琪： ……

寬： 我無呃你，我同佢真係無嘢架。以前係有……我識你之後同佢就再冇啲咩喇。

琪： 咩呀……

寬： 無繼續喇。我哋喺disco識嘅，佢以前喺深圳做嘢，做寫字樓架……佢已經結咗婚架啦……

琪： 結咗婚……

寬： 唔係呀……我哋無一齊之後佢至同第二個結咗婚。

我哋嗰陣都好似幾認真咁，講到結婚但係我唔想，差唔多時間我又識咗你，我咪同佢算囉。應該話我避咗佢……又打電話又send短訊嚟，所以我有時唔敢聽電話……我唔係一腳踏兩船呀，我就係唔想所以我避佢。（停。）可能我知道佢太認真所以我驚。

琪 對一個人「真」都要驚，咁假點算。

寬 係。我唔敢見佢……我知道自己有對佢真嘅時候，我反而唔知點去做。又或者係因為佢係大陸人。好似唔知點去……

琪： 佢係咩嘢人有關係咩？

寬： 係……總之我對佢唔住……我唔理人，阿媽係咁…佢又係咁…對你都係………

（一頓。）

QI   …

KUAN   I didn't lie to you. There was nothing between us. We used to be… There hasn't been anything between us since I met you.

QI   What?

KUAN   We broke up. We met at the disco. She used to work in Shenzhen. She worked in an office… She's married…

QI   Married…

KUAN   No… After we broke up, she married someone else. We seemed to be quite serious at the time. We talked about marriage but I didn't want to. Around that time, I met you, so I broke up with her. The truth is, I avoided her… She called me and sent me text messages. That's why sometimes I didn't answer the phone… I wasn't two-timing you. I didn't want to see her again. That's why I avoided her. (*Pause.*) Maybe I got scared because she was so serious.

QI   You were scared to be serious. What if you wanted to play around?

KUAN   Yeah. I didn't dare see her… I didn't know what to do when things started getting serious. Maybe I didn't know what to do because she's from China…

QI   What does her being from China have to do with it?

KUAN   I know… I was shitty to her… I never care about other people. I'm like that to mom, to her and to you…

            (*A moment.*)

琪：　　　你有冇愛過佢？姓郭嗰個？

寬：　　　……有……我依家可以話係有，不過嗰陣我唔
　　　　　當自己係有。

琪：　　　你覺得自己有！？

寬：　　　已經過咗去，琪。前幾日佢嚟香港搵過我，咁
　　　　　耐都無呀就係呢一次。因為我搞到件事不了了
　　　　　之就算。佢要嚟一個了斷……仲買咗隻鮑魚飯
　　　　　嚟俾我做lunch……

　　　　　（一頓。）

寬：　　　我唔想衰多次。我對佢係真，但係過咗喇。我
　　　　　知道我依家對你都係……

琪：　　　咩呀……

寬：　　　愛你，真架。

琪：　　　……愛一個人唔會走咗去架……

寬：　　　我知我知，我應該早啲嚟搵你……

琪：　　　我係話……

　　　　　（琪的電話響起，琪看來電顯示後按停響聲，
　　　　　再看著寬。）

　　　　　（琪的電話又再響起，琪看電話又按停響聲放
　　　　　回衫袋，沉思一下。）

QI	Did you love her? That Guo woman?
KUAN	…Yeah… I can say I did now. But at the time, I pretended I didn't.
QI	You think you loved her?
KUAN	Qi, it's over. She was back in Hong Kong a few days ago. She came to see me. This was the only time ever. She wanted closure because I left it messy… She bought me an abalone for lunch…
	(*A moment.*)
KUAN	I don't want to screw up again. What I felt about her was real. But that's over now. What I feel about you is…
QI	What?
KUAN	Love. It's real.
QI	When you love someone, you don't disappear.
KUAN	I know. I know. I should have come for you earlier.
QI	What I mean is…
	(*Qi's phone rings. She looks at the display and then stops the ringing. Looks at Kuan.*)
	(*Qi's phone rings again. She looks at it, stops the ringing and returns it to her pocket. She thinks deeply.*)

琪： 　　　（*打破沉默*）……不如你……

　　　（*琪的電話又再響起，這刻琪不再動，電話繼續響。*）

　　　（*大口提著兩個膠袋宵夜緩緩步入，停下，再把自己手上的手提電話按一下，琪的電話響聲停止。*）

　　　（*三人互望。停頓。*）

大： 　　　（*對琪*）我一路行過嚟……以為你……以為有人搞你……

　　　（*停頓。*）

　　　（*寬走向大口，又停步，最後掉頭走去。琪和大口互望。*）

　　　（*此場完。*）

QI   (*Breaking the silence*)…Why don't you…

            (*Qi's phone rings again. This time Qi doesn't move. The phone continues to ring.*)

            (*Da Kou saunters in with two plastic bags. He stops and presses a button on his mobile phone. Qi's phone stops ringing.*)

            (*The three of them look at each other. Pause.*)

DA   (*To Qi*) I was walking over… I thought you… I thought someone was bothering you…

            (*Pause.*)

            (*Kuan approaches Da Kou. Stops. Finally, he turns around and exits. Qi and Da Kou look at each other.*)

            (*End of scene.*)

第十七場：深圳桑拿店門外

（*忠從桑拿店出來，手上有一個膠袋和一個印有『深圳市收容教育所……貴重物品保管袋』字樣的紙袋。講著電話。*）

忠： 揼緊骨點聽電話呀，你唔好咁「嘟黎」得唔得…「韞」咗成兩個禮拜，都要沖個涼食餐飯架，咁你都嘈嘅……喂呀……（*突然很大聲對電話*）……你做乜忟啫……你顧住肚裡便嗰個呀（*明顯是要避開對方的大罵把電話放在肚腩不聽，一頓，再重聽電話。*）……Sorry 囉……（*對方已收線。*）喂喂……大檸樂嘞今次。

（*袋回電話*）

（*大口穿上一件不合身，很窄的T-shirt出現。*）

忠： 喂，攞番你啲嘢啦！仲有袋衫！（*把手上的紙袋和膠袋逮給大口。*）

大： 頂，唔撚要啦。著咗十幾日仲要咩。（*把膠袋拿過即掉入垃圾箱。*）頂佢個肺都離撚晒譜。唉！咁樣非人生活兩個禮拜，真係揼三粒鐘都補唔番。

SCENE 17 – OUTSIDE THE SHENZHEN SAUNA SHOP

(*Zhong enters from the sauna shop. He carries a plastic bag that reads "Shenzhen Shelter Educational Centre… Valuables". He is speaking on the phone.*)

ZHONG   I can't answer the phone in the middle of a massage. Can't you be more reasonable? He's been locked up for two weeks. He needs a massage and food. What are you complaining about?… Hey… (*Suddenly very loudly*) What's your problem?… Watch out for the little one inside your tummy. (*Obviously, he wants to avoid the shouting from the person on the phone so places the phone on his stomach to avoid hearing it. A moment. Listens again.*) I'm sorry, OK? … (*The person hangs up.*) Hello? Hello?… Am I in trouble this time. (*Places the phone in his pocket.*)

(*Da Kou appears in a very tight T-shirt.*)

ZHONG   Hey, take your stuff. And the bag of clothes. (*Hands the bags to Da Kou.*)

DA   I don't fucking want it. I've been wearing it for two weeks. (*Throws plastic bag into garbage can.*) Fucking unbelievable. (*Sighs.*) What an inhumane existence for two weeks. A three-hour massage wouldn't make up for it.

忠：　　都話陪你捹多粒鐘咯。

大：　　費時你老婆嘈你啦。

忠：　　都嘈咗啦！

大：　　有幾多錢係度？

忠：　　交埋你啲罰款，得番四百幾。

大：　　借埋嚟先，連埋啲衫一次過還啦。

忠：　　（*很認真*）喂，件衫咁窄嘅，你肥咗呀！

大：　　咪就係囉……

忠：　　我是但買架咋！

大：　　仲有呀……你呀……買咗條細碼底褲呀。

忠：　　條底都唔啱？

大：　　好「鏈」窄呀。起碼都「大」啦我！

忠：　　係「大」呀。

大：　　你買咗條細碼呀！

忠：　　大碼！L吖嘛。細碼喺上便嗰格，我攞最下便嗰格嘅。

大：　　（*有點發怒*）你老味細碼嚟架，我去垃圾筒刮番出嚟係細碼你食咗佢吖啦。

忠：　　大碼係L，細碼係S吖嘛！L嚟架。

大：　　（*發怒*）我揾番出嚟你食咗佢！（*衝向垃圾筒*）

忠：　　L咯都話……

重回凡間的凡人 ┃ **168**

ZHONG	I said I'd do another hour's massage with you.
DA	I don't want to hear from your wife.
ZHONG	She already called.
DA	How much money do you have left?
ZHONG	After paying your fine, $400.
DA	Let me have it. I'll return it with the clothes.
ZHONG	(*Very seriously*) Hey, the t-shirt is so tight. You gained weight?
DA	I know…
ZHONG	I just bought something.
DA	Oh yeah… You! Did you buy small underwear?
ZHONG	It doesn't fit?
DA	It's so fucking tight! I need large.
ZHONG	It is large.
DA	You bought small!
ZHONG	Large. "L" for large, right? The small ones were on the top. I took the one at the bottom.
DA	(*Starting to lose his temper*) Fuck you, that ain't no small. I'm digging it out of the garbage. If it says small, I'm gonna cram it down your throat.
ZHONG	Large is "L", small is "S", right? It was an "L".
DA	(*Furious*) I'm digging it out and then shoving it down your throat. (*Rushes to garbage can.*)
ZHONG	I told you. It's "L"…

大： （*很大聲*）係細碼。

忠： 係嘞，細碼喇細喇。

大： （*大口怒視忠*）你老味！係！

忠： 咁……唔啱都唔駛掉咗咗佢嘅，又話臭！仲著呀？窄都著住先囉！

大： 無著呀！

（*靜。*）

忠： 你老竇知唔知。

大： 唔返舖頭成兩個禮拜可以唔知？佢叫我唔好打俾佢！

忠： 你都唔會搵你阿媽啦！

大： 屌，玩嘢咩。幾年都唔見一次，叫佢嚟劫獄呀。如果唔係特首條友搞搞震，駛被人屈足十五日。

忠： 佢要「做好呢份工」啫，都唔駛管埋深圳啩！

大： 裡面啲公安講架。

忠： 呢度大陸呀，你乜都信。

DA	(*Loudly.*) It was an "S".
ZHONG	Fine. It was an "S" then.
DA	(*Looks furiously at Zhong.*) You stupid asshole. Yes!
ZHONG	You don't have to throw it away, even if it doesn't fit. You said yours stinks, you shouldn't wear it. Just wear the new one for the time being, even if it's too tight.
DA	I'm not wearing any.
	(*Silence.*)
ZHONG	Does your father know?
DA	I haven't been back for two weeks. Don't you think he knows? He told me not to call him.
ZHONG	You're not gonna call your mother either?
DA	Fuck. Are you serious? I haven't seen her in years. Should I ask her to break me out of jail? If it wasn't for the Chief Executive, I wouldn't have been locked up for 15 days.
ZHONG	He has to "do his job". He is not responsible for Shenzhen.
DA	The police inside said so.
ZHONG	This is China. Don't believe everything you hear.

大： 總之就入佢數呢鑊嘢。輕鬆下啫我，香港人壓力好大呀！喂，就算係殺人犯都唔可以剝奪我人權！毛巾牙刷都要同人一齊用呀，豬食架啲嘢，仲要迫你「打坐」無得瞓。無理由捉消費者嘅！頂佢個肺！我淨係想個腦袋輕鬆一吓！娛樂場所唔係嚟輕鬆吓要嚟做乜呀。

忠： 早知如此又何必當初呢！

大： 嘖……六合彩唔見我中。今日叫著你血濃於水救急扶危，你仲嚟幸災樂禍！

忠： 有報應架！你唔知咩！

大： ……我唔係好明喎。

忠： 你唔明。你做乜同阿琪咁吖。

（頓。）

大： ……總共幾多錢呀，唉，嗯嗯聲落番去撤返俾你喇……唔該晒嘞，唉，早知唔搵你……

忠： 你做乜咁忟先？

大： 我忟咩？阿寬同你講咗！OK。你個八婆我估你實知架嘞。（憤怒）根本就唔係，都無嘢。

忠： 無嘢……咁你做乜咁內疚咁啫。

大： 我內疚？你都癲線。

忠： 喂，你好難唔令人話你無錯架喎！

DA	I still blame him. Life in Hong Kong is so stressful. I just went for some R&R. Even murderers have rights. I had to share towels and toothbrushes with other people. The food was fit for pigs. And I have to "meditate" and not sleep. There's no reason to arrest the consumers. What assholes. I just wanted to relax and clear my mind. If the entertainment centres aren't for relaxation then what the hell are they for?!
ZHONG	What was the purpose of all this?
DA	I've never won the lottery. I asked you for help today and you're blaming me?
ZHONG	You deserved it.
DA	I don't understand.
ZHONG	Don't you? Why are you with Qi?
	(*A moment.*)
DA	How much money do I owe you? (*Sighs.*) Let's get back to Hong Kong and I'll pay you back… Thanks a lot. (*Sighs.*) I shouldn't have called you…
ZHONG	What are you mad about?
DA	Me mad? Kuan told you. OK. I know you know. (*Angrily*) It's not true. Nothing happened.
ZHONG	Nothing? Then why do you sound so guilty?
DA	Me guilty? You're crazy.
ZHONG	Hey, it's kinda hard to not make you the bad guy.

大： 咩嘢事呀，俾著你吖，食下宵夜傾下偈，死罪呀！

忠： 大肚婆唔理我都上嚟接你，唔係淨係想話你唔啱。阿寬都唔啱。我係唔想邊個傷倒邊個唧。

大： 依家受傷嗰個係我呀，我俾人屈我坐咗十五日監呀。唔通同死黨個女朋友傾幾次偈就要坐監呀。我俾埋個膊頭佢佢都唔要呀。

忠： 咁你唔應該俾件事發生吖嗎。咁啱撞倒呀？！

大： 喂，開頭真係咁啱撞倒㗎。我知講都唔會有人信。唉，我悶咁傾下偈啫。唔通搵你傾咩，兩個麻甩佬肉肉麻呀！你就梗係好啦，返屋企有老婆，仲就嚟有仔有囡，我返去有咩，得幾堵牆。

（*靜。*）

忠： 搞清楚囉，同阿寬講。

大： 點講呀？換轉係你你信唔信呀！

忠： 我信。

大： 同你講都嘥氣！（*突然很認真*）你同阿寬講，我同阿琪真係無嘢㗎。要嬲就嬲佢唔理阿琪啦。我同阿寬無嘢講！

（*大口開始離開。*）

DA   What the hell is this? What would you do? A bite and some chitchat. It's not a crime.

ZHONG   I left my pregnant wife at home to come bail you out. I'm not here just to tell you that you screwed up. Kuan screwed up, too. I just don't want anyone to get hurt.

DA   I'm the one who's hurt now. I was thrown in jail for 15 days. I have to go to jail for talking to my buddy's girlfriend? I gave her my shoulder, but she didn't want it.

ZHONG   Should you have let it happen? It was a coincidence?

DA   It was a coincidence to begin with. I know you won't believe me. (*Sighs.*) I was bored. We talked. Was I supposed to talk with you? You want me to talk to another asshole? That sucks. You're doing OK. Got a wife at home. Got a child on its way. What do I have at home? Just four walls.

          (*Silence.*)

ZHONG   Explain to Kuan. Clear the air.

DA   And say what? Would you believe me if you were him?

ZHONG   Yes, I would.

DA   This is useless. (*Suddenly very serious*) Tell Kuan there was nothing between Qi and me. He should blame himself for ignoring Qi. I have nothing to say to him.

          (*Da Kou begins to leave.*)

忠： 喂……喂……

（*大口不理他。*）

忠： 佢都話係自己唔啱架。

（*大口已消失了。剩下忠一人。良久，大口又慢慢回來。*）

大： 你講吖，咁佢依家點呀？

忠： 佢就係好似乜事都無，咁我先驚。

（*此場完。*）

ZHONG   Hey... Hey...

          (*Da Kou ignores him.*)

ZHONG   He admits that he screwed up.

          (*Da Kou has exited. Zhong is left alone. A long moment. Da Kou slowly returns.*)

DA   So tell me, how is he now?

ZHONG   He pretends nothing is wrong. That's what scares me.

          (*End of scene.*)

第十八場：醫院外 /病房

（*舞台的一邊盡處。寬坐在長椅上，身旁有一個大購物袋，手上拿著DV錄影機，姐拿著麵包一邊食一邊氣沖沖地步入。*）

姐： 買唔買倒呀？

寬： 買咗兩隻。遲兩步收檔添呀。

姐： 唔係度度有得買架好衰架。

（*寬起身，姐坐下一邊食麵包。*）

姐： 唔好上去住。

（*寬又坐下。*）

寬： 照咗話係？

姐： 下畫打嚟，我真係「瓊」咗，忍得我幾辛苦，又唔敢喺公司喊出嚟。

寬： 咁快去到隻腳！？

姐： 唉……停針兩個禮拜都無，仲諗住俾佢回吓氣。

寬： 點同佢講？

姐： 知喇。今朝佢同醫生講話「有啲咩都無所謂可以同佢講」喎！

寬： 佢自己直接問醫生！

姐： 咪係囉，有乜理由同個病人講啫，"port"佢。

<u>SCENE 18 – OUTSIDE THE HOSPITAL/
HOSPITAL WARD</u>

(*Kuan is sitting on a long bench at the far corner of the stage. There is a large shopping bag next to him. He has a DV camera. Sister enters in a hurry while eating a piece of bread.*)

SISTER   Did you get it?

KUAN   I bought two. He was about to close. I just made it.

SISTER   It's really hard to find.

(*Kuan rises. Sister sits and eats.*)

SISTER   Let's not go up yet.

(*Kuan sits.*)

KUAN   The scan was positive.

SISTER   They called this afternoon. I just froze. I had to hold it in. I couldn't cry at work.

KUAN   It's in her legs? So fast!

SISTER   (*Sighs.*) We only stopped chemo two weeks ago. I thought she could rest for a while.

KUAN   How are we going to tell her?

SISTER   This morning she told the doctor to tell her everything.

KUAN   The doctor told her himself?

SISTER   Yeah. How could he tell the patient? We should report him.

寬：　　　多餘！

姐：　　　我多餘！你都真係吖！

　　　　　（頓。）

姐：　　　我跟住打俾佢，佢都無晒心機咁，淨係「哦」、「係呀」咁囉。淨係叫我買兩隻雞，想飲湯喝。其實呢啲雞都唔應該食啦！

寬：　　　佢想食咪由佢囉！

姐：　　　醫生話可能會變得好快，好多都係咁。要有心理準備。

　　　　　（姐突然哭起來，寬給她紙巾，姐又努力收起。）

寬：　　　喂！得啦！唔好喊啦！上去啦！

姐：　　　等陣啦，費事俾佢見到我喊成咁。

寬：　　　咁我上去先嘞。（起身。）

姐：　　　做乜啫。咁唔耐煩。喊吓都唔得咩。你姐夫又係咁衰，嗰個阿媽嚟㗎，無人性㗎咩你哋。

寬：　　　喊啦！喊啦。（坐下。）我陪你！

　　　　　（寬坐著，再移近姐身旁。大聲哭泣的姐慢慢地把頭挨在寬的肩膊上。）

　　　　　（燈轉至舞台另一邊演區的病房，媽坐在床邊的椅上，琪坐在床邊拿著一碗湯。）

| KUAN | That's ridiculous. |
| SISTER | Me, ridiculous? Thanks a lot! |

(A moment.)

SISTER	Then I called her. She was kind of down. Just said, "Uh huh… Yup…" Just told me to buy two chickens. She wanted soup. She shouldn't be eating chicken.
KUAN	Let her eat it if she wants to.
SISTER	The doctor said things could change really fast. Most cases are like that. We have to be prepared.

(Sister cries. Kuan gives her a tissue. She attempts to hold it in.)

KUAN	Hey, stop crying. Let's go up.
SISTER	Wait. I don't want her to see me cry.
KUAN	Then I'll go up first. *(Rises.)*
SISTER	What? Am I taking too much of your time? I can't even cry? Your brother-in-law is the same. She's my mother. You are all so cold-hearted.
KUAN	Then cry! Cry! *(Sits.)* I'll keep you company.

(Kuan sits. He moves closer to Sister. Sister, who has been crying loudly, slowly puts her head on Kuan's shoulder.)

(Lights change. Another side of the stage lights up. It is the hospital ward. Mother is resting in the bed. Qi is by the side of the bed with a bowl of soup.)

媽：　　　聽日你嚟唔嚟呀，我叫工人帶多壺湯俾你吖……

琪：　　　日頭嚟吖吓，我夜晚至飛之嘛……

媽：　　　喏啦，帶上飛機飲。

琪：　　　水唔上得飛機㗎。

媽：　　　係……呀係……

琪：　　　……我聽日嚟飲吖。好熱……
　　　　　（仍手持著湯。）

媽：　　　攤一陣先啦。（頓。）工人日日都攞一大壺
　　　　　嚟，我都飲唔晒……

琪：　　　其實我真係有湯飲㗎。

媽：　　　你自己煲呀……

琪：　　　返阿媽度飲咪有囉！

媽：　　　嗰邊淨得啲雪藏嘢邊好食㗎……呀，唔係，有
　　　　　唐人街，呵！

琪：　　　係呀！不過香港都有好多好嘢嘅。

　　　　　（二人笑。）

琪：　　　總之我聽日走之前嚟飲湯啦。

媽：　　　好呀。你真係有心！

琪：　　　唔好客氣，我橫掂都一個人，好free嘅。

媽：　　　你有無諗過返去阿爸阿媽度呀？

MOTHER	Are you coming tomorrow? I'll ask the maid to bring another bowl of soup.
QI	I'll come during the day. I'm flying in the evening…
MOTHER	Good, take some soup onto the plane.
QI	I can't take liquids onboard.
MOTHER	Oh… really?
QI	I'll come and drink soup tomorrow. It's hot.. (*Still holding soup.*)
MOTHER	Wait a while. (*A moment.*) The maid brings a big jug every day. I can't finish it…
QI	I drink soup at home, too.
MOTHER	You make it yourself?
QI	My mother makes it.
MOTHER	They use frozen food over there. How good can it be?… Oh, right. They have Chinatown there, right?
QI	Yes. But the food is still much better in Hong Kong.
	(*They laugh.*)
QI	I'll come and drink some soup tomorrow before I leave.
MOTHER	OK. You're so thoughtful.
QI	It's nothing. I'm alone. I'm free.
MOTHER	Have you thought about going back to your parents'?

琪： 吓！

（頓。）

媽 你阿爸阿媽實會好開心！

琪： 或者啦……

媽： 做父母幾時都想啲仔囡喺身邊嘅。你自己一個喺香港咁耐，佢哋咪就掛你咁耐囉！

琪： 咁我都成日飛返去見佢哋……

媽： 點同呢。唔同架。

琪： 係嘅！

媽： 一個人……好悶架！

琪： 留喺度係我自己揀。（頓）我諗唔鍾意一樣嘢好容易，但係鍾意嘅話我信一個理由就夠。

媽： 我哋以前做女嗰陣無咁多道理。你係人仔囡就俾人養，嫁咗去人哋屋企就係人哋嘅人，生咗仔就要養大佢，就連佢哋啲仔囡都擔心埋佢。無得解，就係咁架咯。

我同阿寬老竇就係坐埋見過一次就一世。佢喺香港做嘢，我喺鄉下等佢。話就話有家婆大伯啲人一齊住，但係都係覺得一個人，連同第啲男人講多句都怕有人講。哈，就係咁過囉。

QI   Huh?

(*A moment.*)

MOTHER   Your parents would be so happy.

QI   Maybe.

MOTHER   All parents want their children by their sides. They must have been missing you all this time while you were in Hong Kong.

QI   I always fly back to see them…

MOTHER   That's different.

QI   You're right.

MOTHER   It's lonely by yourself.

QI   Staying here was my choice. (*A moment.*) It's easy to dislike something. But to like something, all I need is one reason.

MOTHER   We didn't talk so much logic when we were young. We all take care of our own children. When we marry, we belong to someone else. You raise your children, but you also worry about their children. There's no way to explain it. It's a fact of life.

I only met Kuan's father one time before we got married. He worked in Hong Kong and I stayed in the village. I lived with my in-laws but I felt like I was alone. I couldn't even talk with other men. Before I knew it, that had become my entire life.

而家……啲人郁吓就離婚，離完又結，一間屋家爺仔嬲個個都唔同姓都有。

係！個個都想揀到最好，而家可以！不過到頭來都唔知想要乜。

（*靜。*）

琪： 其實我都有諗過返加拿大……或者等遲啲先……

媽： 好，總之你未走，咪嚟飲湯囉。

琪： 唔，你快啲出院返屋企我就上去飲你煲嗰啲。

媽： 好，煲雞湯！

琪： 你唔食得雞架！

媽： 依家乜都食得……

（*琪把手上的湯飲完。*）

（*燈再轉回到寬和姐的長椅，姐手上仍拿著未食完的麵包。一陣靜默。*）

寬： 阿囡嚟唔嚟睇婆婆呀？

姐： 聽日又話默書。係喎……唔記得！要叫佢老豆睇住佢默一次（*找電話*）。

寬： 佢知唔知婆婆咁呀？

These days, people get divorced at the drop of a hat. They get divorced and then get re-married. Everyone in the family has a different surname.

Yes, everyone tries to make the right choice. But that isn't easy if you don't know what you want.

(*Silence.*)

QI   Actually, I thought about going back to Canada... Maybe later.

MOTHER   Well, as long as you're here, come and drink soup.

QI   Get well and I'll come to your house for soup.

MOTHER   OK. Chicken soup.

QI   I thought you couldn't eat chicken.

MOTHER   I'm eating everything I want from now on...

(*Qi finishes the soup she's holding.*)

(*Lights change back to Kuan and Sister on the bench. Sister is still holding the piece of bread. Silence.*)

KUAN   Is your daughter coming to see her grandmother?

SISTER   She has dictation tomorrow. Oh yeah... I almost forgot. I have to ask her dad to review her dictation. (*Looks for phone.*)

KUAN   Does she know about her grandmother?

姐： 　　（*遲疑*）梗係唔同佢講啦，嚇親佢咩？（*對電話*）喂，爸爸，仲未返倒呀……呀囝聽日默書，你記得同佢默一次呀，係呀……唔係佢又「乍乍帝」呀……係咁啦。（*收線*）

　　（*靜。*）

寬： 　　養大個細路真係好辛苦。

姐： 　　係咁架啦，讀書做嘢結婚生仔湊大佢咪退休囉。你話做人幾辛苦！

寬： 　　你同姐夫結咗婚幾耐？

姐： 　　個囝咁大咪加多三年囉。

寬： 　　姐夫愛唔愛你？

姐： 　　……咩呀？

寬： 　　你呢？

姐： 　　我咩啫！（*拿出水飲*）做乜講埋哩啲嘢啫……

寬： 　　你哋多唔多偈傾？定無嘢講？嗌交？唔理大家淨係做自己嘢？

姐： 　　佢又返工我又返工，又要顧個囝。總之無病無痛唔駛擔心咪就好好囉。唉……個個都係咁架啦……咪愛囉，乜唔愛啫。

寬： 　　……老豆唔知愛唔愛阿媽呢……

　　（*兩人靜下來。*）

姐： 　　寬呀……你諗著點呀……

SISTER	(*Hesitates.*) Of course I haven't told her. That will scare her. (*To phone*) Hello, honey? You're not home yet?... Our daughter has dictation tomorrow. Remember to review it with her. Yes... Otherwise she'll make excuses... That's all. (*Hangs up.*)
	(*Silence.*)
KUAN	It's so hard to raise children.
SISTER	That's the way it is. School, work, marriage, have children, raise children, and then you retire. Life is hard!
KUAN	How long have you been married?
SISTER	My daughter's age, plus three years.
KUAN	Does your husband love you?
SISTER	What?
KUAN	And you?
SISTER	And me what? (*Takes out water to drink.*) Why are you asking me that?
KUAN	Do you talk much? Or is there nothing to say? Do you fight? Or do you do your own thing?
SISTER	We both work. We have to take care of our daughter. As long as everyone is well and there's nothing to worry about, it's fine. (*Sighs.*) That's the way it is... Of course I love him. Why not!
KUAN	... I wonder if dad loved mom...
	(*They are quiet.*)
SISTER	Kuan, what are you going to do?

寬： 咩點呀！

姐： 今晚過嚟瞓，返去又遠，又係一個人。

寬： 唔駛。我返去得架啦。姐呀，唔該晒你，阿媽喺你嗰邊……

姐： 發神經咩！唔該！唔做邊個做呀，大家都要理架，想做就幾遠都會做，唔想……住隔離都無用！

（寬電話響起，姐一邊把食物食完。）

寬： 喂……佢打嚟……媽……到咗喇上緊嚟……喺樓下 ……買咗喇。吓……哦……我哋上嚟啦。

（寬收線，姐起身行了幾步，發現寬仍站著。）

姐： 做咩？你唔好嚇我呀！

寬： 無嘢。行啦！

（燈光轉變至媽的床邊，寬和姐步入病房，琪已離開。）

姐： 阿琪呢，又話嚟咗 ……

寬： 係囉……媽……你話佢……

媽： 做乜咁遲啫，佢啱啱走之嘛，無見到佢咩？

姐： 無喎……（拿起琪留下的書。）邊個俾本書你呀……

KUAN	What?
SISTER	Stay at my place tonight. Your place is too far. And you're alone.
KUAN	Nah… I am fine at home. Sister, thank you for taking care of mom…
SISTER	Don't be stupid. Thank me? Who else can we count on? We all have to care. If you care, it doesn't matter how far away you are. If you don't care, it wouldn't matter if you lived next door.

(*Kuan's phone rings. Sister finishes eating.*)

| KUAN | Hello?… It's her… Mom? We're here. We're coming up… We're downstairs… We got it. Huh? … Oh… We'll come up. |

(*Kuan hangs up. Sister rises and walks a few steps. She realizes that Kuan is still standing.*)

SISTER	What is it? Don't scare me.
KUAN	Nothing. Let's go.

(*Lights change to Mother's bed. Kuan and Sister enter hospital ward. Qi has left.*)

SISTER	Where is Qi? She said she'd come…
KUAN	Yeah… Mom, you said she…
MOTHER	Why are you so late? She just left. Didn't you see her?
SISTER	No… (*Picks up the book that Qi left.*) Whose book is this? Yours?

媽： 　……阿琪攞咗啲果汁嚟俾我飲……

姐： 　……哦，食生果就點都係對身體好嘅。（*把書給寬。*）

寬： 　（*對媽*）真係啱啱走？

媽： 　我都叫佢坐多陣佢又話唔好……

寬： 　或者佢真係有嘢做呢……

媽： 　佢話返加拿大喇！

寬： 　係咩！

　　　（*一頓。*）

寬： 　啲果汁好唔好飲呀……媽？

姐： 　唔落去睇吓……或者仲等緊車啫……

寬： 　（*對媽*）呀……係呀……買咗雞喇。買兩咗隻，喺旺角買架。

媽： 　去到旺角？

寬： 　家姐話嗰度有吖嗎……

姐： 　得啦，買咗就得啦。

寬： 　（*對媽*）你想點整呀啲雞……係咪煲湯呀……煲湯你飲好唔好！聽日下晝我嚟同你食飯吖。不如煮埋雞飯。兩樣都整好唔好？

姐： 　吓，食咁多？得唔得呀……

MOTHER   Qi brought me some juice.

SISTER   Oh…Fruits are always good for the body. (*Gives Kuan the book.*)

KUAN   (*To Mother*) She just left?

MOTHER   I told her to stay a while longer but she said no…

KUAN   Maybe she's busy…

MOTHER   She said she's going back to Canada.

KUAN   Really?

            (*A moment.*)

KUAN   Is the juice good, Mom?

SISTER   Go and check downstairs… Maybe she's waiting for a cab…

KUAN   (*To Mother*) Oh… Yeah… I bought the chicken. I bought two. Bought them in Mongkok.

MOTHER   In Mongkok?

KUAN   Sister said they have them there…

SISTER   Right… You bought them. That's fine.

KUAN   (*To Mother*) How do you want them cooked? You want soup? Shall we make soup for you? I can come here to have lunch with you tomorrow. Let's make chicken rice. Let's cook both, all right?

SISTER   So much food? Can you…

寬： 咪咁孤寒啦，一半一半咪得囉。

姐： 講咩你，我孤寒，佢唔食得咁多雞架……

寬： （突然有點怒氣）是但啦……

姐： 你都傻架……

媽： （發脾氣）嗨，咁都好嘈，煮晒佢。煲湯！擺埋兩個雞脾煮飯，一餐食唔晒食兩餐。依家乜都食得喇！

（此場完。）

KUAN   Don't be so stingy. Just cook half portions.

SISTER Me stingy? Mom can't eat so much chicken…

KUAN   (*Suddenly a little angry*) Whatever…

SISTER You're so stupid…

MOTHER (*Throws a tantrum. Sighs.*) Stop it! Cook it all. Soup. Cook chicken rice with both chickens. If I can't finish it in one meal, I'll eat it for the next meal. I am eating everything I want now.

        (*End of scene.*)

第十九場：琪家樓下

（*琪出現，寬入。兩人靜默對望。*）

寬： 你要返加拿大？

琪： （*頓*）係……

寬： 返加拿大？

琪： 唔。

寬： 下星期就走！

琪： 唔。

（*靜。*）

琪： ……你同大口好多年friend……

寬： 唔好講……好唔好呀……

琪： 但係我想講。

寬： OK！

琪： 其實……算啦，都係唔好講。

寬： OK！

琪： 不過同佢做朋友OK嘅。

寬： 唔唔！

琪： ……你哋……仲係好朋友！？

（*一頓。*）

寬： 係。

琪： 有啲嘢唔會話無就無嘅，唔係話撳個制就得。

SCENE 19 - OUTSIDE OF QI'S RESIDENCE

(Qi appears. Kuan enters. They look at each other in silence.)

KUAN   You're going back to Canada?

QI   *(A moment.)* Yeah…

KUAN   You're going back to Canada?

QI   Uh huh.

KUAN   Next week?

QI   Uh huh.

       (Silence.)

QI   …You and Da Kou have been friends for years…

KUAN   Don't. Please.

QI   But I have something to say.

KUAN   OK!

QI   Actually… Forget it. Let's just leave it.

KUAN   OK!

QI   He's a good guy. A good friend.

KUAN   Uh huh.

QI   …Are you guys… still friends?

       (A moment.)

KUAN   Yes.

QI   There are some things that just don't go away. You can't just switch it off.

寬：　　係囉。我哋唔會撤個制啲嘢就會無咗。唔會。

（靜。）

寬：　　咁我哋係咪就咁就完？

琪：　　之前我覺得你唔好，但係而家我唔係咁諗。因為你都可以做你想做嘅⋯⋯

寬：　　你係咪答緊我？

琪：　　我係答緊你。

寬：　　你講架，我哋唔會撤個制啲嘢就會無咗。唔會。

琪：　　所以我要講清楚，我就係唔想好似你咁唔聲唔聲走咗去。

寬：　　（有點激動）因為我以前咁對你係咪⋯⋯我擺埋你一邊？

琪：　　唔係因為「以前」⋯⋯

寬：　　我而家理喇，我會喺埋家姐度瞓架，我盡量陪阿媽架喇⋯⋯

琪：　　（也激動起來）如果我唔係返加拿大，你都唔會而家搵我架！嗰晚見到大口出現你都係走咗去，你根本唔想理。你唔想理！你知唔知呀！

寬：　　所以你就咁對番我！

琪：　　寬，邊個都無傷害倒邊個，要錯就大家都錯，只係timing問題⋯⋯

KUAN	Yeah. We can't just switch off our friendship. No.
	(*Silence.*)
KUAN	So is it over for us?
QI	I used to think you were a creep. But I don't think that anymore. Because you are free to do what you want…
KUAN	Are you answering my question?
QI	I'm answering your question.
KUAN	You just can't switch it off. You said it. You can't.
QI	That's why I want to make it clear. I don't want to just leave without being clear, like you.
KUAN	(*A little emotional.*) Because that's how I used to treat you, right? I put you on the side?
QI	Not because you "used to"…
KUAN	I care now. I'm going to stay with my sister. I want to be with my mom as much as possible…
QI	(*Also a little emotional.*) If I wasn't returning to Canada, you wouldn't even have come to see me. That night when you saw Da Kou, you left. You don't want to care. You don't want to. You know that?
KUAN	So that's why you are treating me like this now?
QI	Kuan, we didn't hurt each other. We're both at fault. It was just bad timing…

寬： 唔係架…唔係架…其實我哋仲可以……

琪： ……「其實」都過咗去嘅……以後係點我唔
知……邊個知……不過而家我想搞清楚自己想
點。

寬： 我知係因為我……

琪： （截他）唔係淨係因為你……都唔係因為邊
個…真係唔係…唔係…

（一頓。）

琪： 有一日我喺機艙望出窗口，我問自己：「其實
我喺個天度飛嚟飛去係做乜架？」

一直我都認為自己有好多嘢要去做，所以唔理
屋企四圍去。

趁後生吖嗎，唔做幾時做呀係咪！香港好
玩……我留喺度囉！我遇到你我留喺度！愛
情！事業！生活！咩都好似好應該咁！其實我
哋只係為自己搵個講法，連daddy mummy都
幫我哋講埋一份，因為佢哋都要同自己講唔可
以阻住我哋架嗎。咁我哋就無憂無慮咁喺天度
飛嚟飛去，自由自在。（頓）我細個有一次去
公園玩，以為daddy mummy一定會坐定定喺
張凳度等我，但係到我玩到忘咗形嘅時候再望
返過去，至發現張凳度無咗人，佢哋唔見咗。
你驚唔驚呀！有啲人珍惜我哋，需要我哋，我
哋唔好辜負佢。我哋不如返返去最需要我哋嘅
人身邊啦。真架，你都一樣！（頓）我哋其實
真係唔需要對方。起碼依家係。

（長靜。）

（寬非常平靜。）

KUAN   No. No. Actually, I think we still can…

QI   "Actually", it's all over… I don't know what the future holds… No one knows… But right now I just need to figure out what I'm feeling.

KUAN   I know it's because of me…

QI   (*Interrupts him.*) It's not just because of you… It's not anyone in particular. Really, it's not.

        (*A moment.*)

QI   One day, I was staring out the window in the cabin. I asked myself, "What am I doing flying all over the sky?" I always thought I had lots of things I needed to do, so I neglected my home and went everywhere. Do it while I'm young, right? What am I waiting for! Hong Kong is fun… so I stayed here. I met you and I stayed here. Love! Career! Life! Everything seemed necessary. But we were just looking for an excuse. Even my parents were doing the same for us, because they had to tell themselves not to stand in our way. So I could fly around the sky with no worries. Be free. (*A moment.*) When I was little, I went to the park once. I thought my parents would just sit on the park bench and wait for me. But when I was playing intently, I looked over and realized there was no one on the bench. They were gone. I was terrified! There are some people who really need us, who treasure us. We can't let them down. We should go back to the people who need us most. I'm serious. That's what you should do. (*A moment.*) We don't really need each other. At least we don't right now.

        (*Long silence.*)

        (*Kuan is very peaceful.*)

寬： 如果我突然死咗你會點呀？

琪： 你唔明我講乜⋯⋯

寬： 我明。

琪： 咁你做乜咁講⋯⋯

寬： 一個人死咗，唔再喺呢個世界，佢都仲係佢，係會影響倒其他人⋯⋯

琪： 我唔要咁呀！

寬： 你話唔會撤個制就無咗架嗎。

琪： 俾啲時間自己。

寬： （突然大聲）我無時間喇⋯⋯

（寬愈來愈激動。）

寬： 我突然諗唔倒老豆嗰樣。

琪： 寬？

寬： 放心，我唔會去玩死。你講得好好⋯⋯呢幾日我成日諗起老豆⋯⋯一諗起我就打冷震。我返到屋企一出電梯，我就離遠見到佢企喺度個樣！好似佢仲喺度⋯⋯佢本來好好地，點解會突然唔喺度。

琪： 不如同你返屋企先⋯⋯

KUAN	What would you do if I died suddenly?
QI	Do you understand what I said?
KUAN	I do.
QI	Then why are you talking about...
KUAN	When you die, you're not of this world anymore. But you are still you. You can still influence others.
QI	I don't want that.
KUAN	You said you just can't switch it off.
QI	Give yourself time.
KUAN	(*Suddenly very loudly*) I don't have time!
	(*Becomes very emotional.*)
KUAN	I can't remember my father's face.
QI	Kuan?
KUAN	Don't worry. I wouldn't commit suicide. You were right... I've been thinking about my father these last few days... Every time I think about him, I shudder. When I get home, when I get out of the elevator, I see his face, far away from me. It's like he's still there...He was fine! Why did he die?
QI	Let me take you home first...

寬：　　（*有點自言自語*）佢嘅嘢我好多都唔知，我應該同佢傾多啲囉。嗰次同佢睇醫生我仲覺得好煩，我無乜理佢。如果我做多啲⋯⋯佢或者唔會就咁就走咗。但係我無。不過依家⋯⋯我好似覺得同佢好近。但係佢唔會知我而家咁諗。佢點會知啫係咪。

琪：　　（*知道寬不妥*）對唔住⋯⋯我唔應該而家同你講⋯⋯

寬：　　OK！OK！我無嘢⋯⋯（*突然笑起來*）⋯⋯日日都會有人死有人生，哈！其實關我哋咩嘢事！（*突然很認真地*）係關我哋事！佢哋死咗⋯⋯佢哋唔會知有人傷心。仲有嗰啲未出世嘅⋯⋯佢哋都未嚟啲人已經不知幾開心，呀忠就嚟做老竇喇，你睇佢幾開心。但係佢嗰個「仔」定「囡」會唔會知呀忠咁開心呀？佢哋唔知。我老竇走咗⋯⋯佢知唔知阿媽會搞成咁吖。係囉，阿媽而家咁，可能就係因為老竇唔喺度。但係唔喺度嘅人，點會知呢！係咪呀？

琪：　　寬⋯⋯寬⋯⋯

寬：　　但係我知⋯⋯我知⋯⋯（*寬突然喊了出來。*）

　　　　（*此場完。*）

KUAN   (*A little to himself*) There is so much about him I don't know. I should have talked more with him. I was annoyed with him that time I had to take him to the doctor. I didn't care about him then. If I had done more…maybe he'd still be here. But I didn't. Now… I feel as if he is very close. But he won't know how I feel now. How could he know?!

QI   (*Realizes there is something wrong with Kuan.*) Sorry… I shouldn't have talked about this with you right now…

KUAN   OK! OK! I'm fine… (*Suddenly laughs.*) People die every day, right? Actually it wasn't my fault. (*Suddenly very serious.*) Yes, it was my fault. They're dead. They don't know if someone is missing them. How about babies who aren't born yet?… They haven't even arrived but they've already made someone happy. Zhong is going to be a father soon. See how happy he is. But does his son or daughter know how happy he is? They don't know. My father is dead. Does he know how my mother is? Yes. Maybe my mother's illness was caused by my father's death. But the dead never know, right?

QI   Kuan… Kuan…

KUAN   But I know… I know.. (*Suddenly cries.*)

   (*End of scene.*)

第二十場：靈養院

（媽在床上熟睡著，頭上戴著冷帽。鼻上有一條氧氣喉插著。寬手持一部爛了的DV攝錄機，左右分別是支離破碎的觀景器和DV機主體，似乎DV機已無法再用，他看看手上的DV機，又看熟睡的媽。）

（一會兒後，寬隨便把DV機放下，走到床邊叫醒媽媽。）

寬：　　媽……媽……媽！

（媽醒來看見寬。）

寬：　　媽！

媽：　　嚟咗呀。

（寬媽的精神狀況明顯比之前虛弱，帶點呆滯。）

寬：　　係。

媽：　　幾點呀依家？

寬：　　三點兩個字。

媽：　　我以為有五點，工人攞飯嚟。

寬：　　無，三點幾咋。

媽：　　啱啱嚟呀。

寬：　　一陣啦。

媽：　　你嚟咪叫醒我囉。

寬：　　我諗你都瞓咗唔係好耐咪由你瞓陣添囉。

SCENE 20 – NURSING HOME

(Mother is fast asleep in bed. She wears a wool cap and has oxygen tubing on her nose. Kuan carries a broken DV camera. Around him are broken pieces of the viewfinder and some other parts of the DV camera. It appears that the DV camera is no longer functional. He looks at the DV camera in his hand, then he looks at sleeping Mother.)

(A while later, Kuan casually puts down the DV camera. Walks over to the bed and wakes Mother.)

KUAN   Mom... Mom... Mom...

(Mother wakes up and sees Kuan.)

KUAN   Mom.

MOTHER   What time is it?

KUAN   Ten past three.

MOTHER   I thought it was five. That's when they bring dinner.

KUAN   No. It's only three.

MOTHER   You just came?

KUAN   A while ago.

MOTHER   You should have woken me up.

KUAN   I thought you'd just fallen asleep, so I thought I'd let you rest.

媽：　　叫醒我吖嘛，都唔想瞓咁多，我都怕日頭瞓咗夜晚瞓唔倒，嘿，又唔係，都係咁瞓，總之成日都瞓得。

寬：　　食咗啲藥，就係要你休息吖嘛！

媽：　　係囉，成日都瞓架喎。咁得意架喎。

寬：　　呢度靜呀，威爾斯又人多又迫。

　　　　（*靜。*）

　　　　（*此時飾演忠的演員出現舞台某角落。*）

媽：　　……對面床嗰個仲好瞓，兩個禮拜咯我都無見佢醒過，唔知係咪咁啹我醒佢又瞓喇。

寬：　　呢度都幾舒服吖，我地又隨時嚟都得。

媽：　　係，啲姑娘都好，成日都嚟睇下你，問痛唔痛呀，「如果痛就叫我地，知唔知呀」。

　　　　（*靜。*）

寬：　　咁你有無覺痛呀？

媽：　　瞓咗就唔知，有時醒咗就有啲啲。

寬：　　唔好忍阿媽。

媽：　　得架啦。啲嗎啡會愈食愈多架。大便都難去啲。

寬：　　你有無大便呀？

MOTHER	Wake me up. I don't want to sleep so much. If I sleep during the day, I won't sleep at night. It doesn't matter. I just end up sleeping all day.
KUAN	The medication is supposed to help you sleep.
MOTHER	I know. It makes you sleep all day. Strange.
KUAN	It's quiet here. Prince of Wales is too crowded.

(*Silence.*)

(*At this time, the actor who plays Zhong comes on stage.*)

MOTHER	…The one in the bed across from me can really sleep. I haven't seen her awake in two weeks. I wonder if she wakes up when I sleep.
KUAN	It's comfortable here. We can come to see you any time.
MOTHER	Yes. The nurses are very nice. They check on you all the time. They ask if I'm in pain. "If you're in pain, just call us, OK?"

(*Silence.*)

KUAN	So are you in pain?
MOTHER	I don't feel it if I'm sleeping. Sometimes when I wake up, I hurt a little.
KUAN	Don't just endure it.
MOTHER	I won't. They're increasing the morphine. My bowels won't move.
KUAN	You don't have bowel movements?

媽： 今朝都有少少。坐盤囉。

寬： 咪好囉，有入有出就得架喇。

媽： 啲呀嬸都好好。

寬： 啡色嗰兩粒藥係幫你大便架。要去就叫呀嬸，唔好忍呀，知唔知。

媽： 得。我會，總之唔好痛就得架喇。死唔緊要，我最怕痛。

（*靜*。）

（*飾演大口的演員出現舞台另一角落。*）

（*媽發現DV機。*）

媽： 你頭先又影呀，

寬： 無影呀，跌爛咗喇。

媽： 都話唔好影咯。咁嘅樣有乜好影吖。

寬： 無呀。

媽： 你快啲掉晒佢添呀。

寬： 你都鍾意影相架。

媽： 依家咁嘅樣有乜好影，頭髮又甩晒。

寬： 你個頭都唔知幾靚，又圓又無話一忽忽。

媽： 無晒啲頭髮，核突到死。

寬： 你啲頭髮出返黎喇。

MOTHER	A little this morning. With a bedpan.
KUAN	That's good. As long as you have some movement.
MOTHER	The nurse's aides are very kind.
KUAN	The two brown pills are for bowel movements. If you need to go, call the nurse's aides. Don't endure the pain, OK?
MOTHER	I know. I won't. I just don't want any pain. Death is not a problem. I just hate pain.
	(*Silence.*)
	(*The actor playing Da Kou enters on another corner of the stage.*)
	(*Mother discovers the DV camera.*)
MOTHER	You were filming just now?
KUAN	No, it fell and broke.
MOTHER	I told you not to bother. What's the point with me looking like this.
KUAN	I didn't.
MOTHER	Throw it away.
KUAN	But you like taking pictures.
MOTHER	I don't want to, looking like this. I have no hair left.
KUAN	Your head is beautiful. It's round and even.
MOTHER	No hair. So ugly.
KUAN	Your hair will grow back.

媽：　　係咩？

寬：　　都話啲化療藥一停就出番架啦，依家咪出番囉。我剃光頭就難睇。後便呢度扁嘅。你都唔知幾靚。

媽：　　我老竇就係。我好細個佢就光頭。啲人仲話佢有錢佬相添。

寬：　　我知。

媽：　　你又知，你都無見過佢。

寬：　　有張相婆婆同佢一齊架嘛……

媽：　　我同你家姐講咗，第時用我擺回鄉證嗰張相，佢知架喇。

　　　　（靜。）

寬：　　……你頭先扯晒鼻鼾，瞓得好好呀？

媽：　　好大聲呀？

寬：　　我埋到你身邊至聽倒啫。

媽：　　我扯鼻鼾咩？

寬：　　我叫醒你嗰陣你好似發緊夢，係咪呀。

媽：　　一瞓就發夢，不過一醒就唔記得，我瞓緊知道發緊夢喎，都話要記住，但係醒咗呢就唔記得架喇。係記得發到你老竇拖住我手影咗張相。咁得意。一瞓就有夢發架喇。

MOTHER	What?
KUAN	After chemo, the hair will grow back. It's growing back now. I wouldn't look very good bald. My head is flat back here. Yours is beautiful.
MOTHER	My father's head was nice. He was already bald when I was very young. People said he looked like a wealthy man.
KUAN	I know.
MOTHER	How do you know? You never met him.
KUAN	There is a photo of him and grandma…
MOTHER	I told your sister, I want to use the photo on my home return permit. She knows the one.
	(*Silence.*)
KUAN	…You were snoring just now. Did you sleep well?
MOTHER	Was I loud?
KUAN	I could only hear it when I was near you.
MOTHER	I was snoring?
KUAN	You seemed to be dreaming when I woke you. Were you?
MOTHER	I dream as soon as I fall asleep. But I can't remember the dreams. I know when I'm dreaming. I tell myself to remember it, but I don't remember anything when I wake up. I just remember I had a dream of your father holding my hand during a photo. Funny. I dream as soon as I fall asleep.

寬： 我尋晚都發咗個夢，發夢返咗去牛頭角，好真架，醒咗個心仲跳到仆仆聲。

媽： 發惡夢呀。

寬： 又唔算係……發夢我返咗去下村……

（寬開始對媽講夢的故事，他像給入睡前的小朋友講故事一樣，自己也興致勃勃。）

（飾演姐的演員再出現在另一角落。）

寬： ……我好細個嘅……好似小學啩……我喺天度飛，但係呢……就被張棉胎捲住……細個嗰陣嗰張紅色一個個腰果花嗰張呢……好似捲壽司咁樣俾佢捲住，手腳都唔郁得，得個頭可以拎離拎去咁喺天度飛。飛得好快架。一路飛就見到以前樓下街市……樓下間辦館……嗰間冰室……公園仔……仲有個「sir」滑梯，見過嘅嘢。然後我「蓬」一聲就飛咗返以前屋企，浮咗喺天花板度。我喺天花度望落去……我哋以前間屋真係好細……見倒你同老竇瞓晒，我同家姐就瞓係嗰張梳化床，防火膠板木嗰張呢。

KUAN   I had a dream last night too. I dreamed I went back to Ngau Tau Kok. It seemed so real. My heart was pounding when I woke up.

MOTHER   A nightmare?

KUAN   Not really… I dreamed I went back to the lower village…

         (*Kuan begins to tell Mother the story of his dream. It is like a story one tells a child at bedtime. He becomes animated.*)

         (*The actor who plays Sister enters on another corner of the stage.*)

KUAN   …I was very young… I think it was primary school… I was flying in the sky. But I got wrapped up by a quilt… The quilt we had when I was little, the one with the paisley print… It rolled me up like sushi. I couldn't move my arms or legs. I could only move my head as I flew through the sky. I was flying very fast. From above, I could see the market that used be on our street… the offices… the coffee shop… the park… and the slide. All the things I saw on our street when I was little. Then – poof! – I was back in our old house. I was floating on the ceiling. I looked down… Our house was really small… I saw you and dad sleeping. Sister and I were sleeping on the sofa bed, the one made from Formica. I saw myself sleeping there. I could see it all so clearly.

我就係攞住嗰張紅色一個個腰果花嘅棉胎。

好清楚架，見到自己瞓喺嗰度。

（*燈光慢慢轉變，只看見寬，寬愈講愈專注夢境*）

突然間⋯⋯「蓬」⋯⋯我由天花板跌落去，跌落去自己度。好快，係好快架！嗰吓離心力好勁，好似玩海盜船咁樣。我就入咗我自己度。（*他好像在很高的地方向下望*）「蓬」一下！（*做出從高處跌下來的動作，急速地呼吸，很驚的樣子*）就係咁！

好似靈魂出竅依家返嚟自己嗰身度。

然後我擘大眼，我好靜咁瞓喺我個被竇，我好似去完唔知邊度返番嚟。我望去你哋張床，見到你同老竇瞓緊覺，好靜。家姐又係，好平靜，咩事都無，除咗嗰吓離心力嚇到我「迫仆迫仆」嘅心跳聲⋯⋯

（*這時寬用手從心口拿出幻想出來的心臟，然後做著心臟在手中跳動的動作。此時台上的其他演員都同樣做著心臟在手中跳動的動作，直至心跳停下來。這一刻琪出現在寬面前。寬看著眼前的琪。*）

寬：　我唔想佢死。

琪：　唔好驚⋯⋯唔係，你可以驚，但係一陣就好嘞。然後你要同自己講，「佢愛我，無論點樣，最後都會無事」。

(*Lights change slowly. We see only Kuan. He becomes immersed in his dream.*)

Suddenly… Poof! … I fell from the ceiling. I fell on top of my own body in the bed. It was fast. Very fast. The force was incredible. Just like the pirate ship ride at Ocean Park. I fell back into my body. (*He seems to be looking down from a great height.*) Poof! (*Performs an action to indicate falling from a great height. He pants. Seems to be scared.*) Just like that! It was like my soul left my body and then returned. Then I opened my eyes. I was very still under my covers. I didn't know where I'd been. I looked at your bed. I saw you asleep with dad. Very quiet. Sister was asleep too. Very peaceful. Nothing was moving, except that the force pulling me down had scared me so much that my heart was pounding, "boom boom… boom boom…" I couldn't hear anything… "Boom boom… boom boom…"

(*Kuan places his hand over his chest and pulls out an imaginary heart. His hand pulses like the pounding heart. At this time, the other actors on the stage perform the same action of the pounding heart with their hands, until the heart stops pounding. At this moment, Qi appears in front of Kuan. He looks at her.*)

KUAN   I don't want her to die.

QI   Don't be afraid… No, you can be afraid. But only for a moment. Then you will have to say to yourself, "She loved me. No matter what happens, it will be fine."

寬：　　　　「佢愛我！」

琪：　　　　非常愛你！

寬：　　　　「無論點樣，最後一定會無事」？

琪：　　　　寬，唔容易架。現實就係咁，有時意想不到，但係我哋可以同佢對抗！我地要同佢一齊。

寬：　　　　……

　　　　　　（*頓。*）

琪：　　　　我都會同自己講，無論點，最後一定會無事。

寬：　　　　你會？

琪：　　　　我會。事情過咗之後我會變得堅強，我會勇敢，因為當我咁樣講既時候，你都會喺我身邊！

　　　　　　（*靜。*）

琪：　　　　多謝你！

寬：　　　　多謝你！

　　　　　　（*琪離開寬面前，最後寬慢慢平靜地望著床上的媽媽。*）

　　　　　　（*燈光回到場景，媽已入睡。*）

寬：　　　　我就醒咗……

　　　　　　（*良久。寬坐著定神地看著他的媽媽，他突然把DV機拿起看一看，然後把它掉入垃圾筒內。*）

KUAN   "She loved me."

QI   Very much.

KUAN   "No matter what happens, it will be fine?"

QI   Kuan, it won't be easy. But this is reality. Sometimes it's unexpected, but we can't fight it. We have to go along with it.

KUAN   …

            (*Pause.*)

QI   I'll also tell myself, no matter what happens, I'll be fine.

KUAN   You will?

QI   I will. When it is all over, I'll be stronger. I'll be braver. Because when I tell myself this, you will be by my side.

            (*Silence.*)

QI   Thank you.

KUAN   Thank you.

            (*Qi leaves Kuan. Finally, Kuan looks peacefully at Mother.*)

            (*Lights change back to the scene. Mother is asleep.*)

KUAN   I woke up…

            (*A while later. Kuan sits motionless, looking at Mother. Suddenly, he looks at the DV camera. He places it in the garbage can.*)

（*此時台上的其他演員已到了媽媽的床前，演員開始扶起飾演媽媽的演員，參扶著送她離場。*）

寬：　最後嘅階段……呼吸更加急速……困難……用力……最大嘅力氣吸一口氣……

姐：　……然後吐出嚟……一吓一吓，噴出嚟啲濕氣喺嗰個透明嘅口罩度……遮住佢個嘴。

忠：　心口起伏好大……有時連續幾吓後就停咗……好似一切已經完成咁。喺以為完結嘅嗰一吓……我心口好似有嚿就要湧出嚟‥

大：　……個鼻好酸……眼淚就嚟要流出嚟嘅時候…… 佢突然又好大力咁吸一啖氣。

琪：　佢心口再一次起伏……然後又好用力咁吐出一口氣。

姐：　咁樣維持咗成三四個鐘頭，跟住有一吓……佢呼完氣出嚟就唔再吸。我望住佢……

忠：　……心諗係咪就係呢吓……

大：　……終於……

琪：　……唔再吸喇……唔再郁……

姐：　……無再郁……所有都停咗……

寬：　……靜止……

（*長停頓。*）

(At this time, other actors come to Mother's bedside. They help carry the actor who was playing Mother off stage.)

KUAN   The last stage... Breathing quickened... It's hard... Try harder... Use your strength to inhale...

SISTER   ... And exhale... Little by little, the moist air is exhaled into the transparent mask... covering her mouth.

ZHONG   Her chest rose and fell sharply... Sometimes it stopped after a few breaths... like that was the end. When I thought it was over... my chest felt like it wanted to burst...

DA   ...I felt a twinge in my nose... When my tears were about to fall... she inhaled deeply.

QI   Her chest rose and fell again... Then she exhaled forcefully.

SISTER   This continued for three or four hours. Then at one point... she exhaled for the last time, and never inhaled again. I looked at her...

ZHONG   ...I thought to myself, is this the breath...

DA   ... Finally...

QI   ...She stopped breathing... She stopped moving...

SISTER   ...She stopped... Everything stopped.

KUAN   ... Silence...

(Long silence.)

寬： 差唔多七個鐘頭，我哋嗰日喺醫院睇住佢七個鐘頭。家姐、姐夫、佢哋嗰女，我哋都圍住床邊睇住佢。我哋咩嘢都做唔倒。我只可以揸住佢隻手望住佢。我有時諗……佢依家知唔知我哋喺度呢。佢係咪會好痛呢……如是者我哋喺醫院陪佢最後嘅七個鐘頭。

（*停頓。*）

寬： 仲有一件事，嗰朝去到醫院，行到電梯門口嘅時候，家姐突然叫住我話：「等等，你背脊有隻嘢」，我停落嚟，好小心咁除咗件外套轉過嚟睇吓。一隻淺粉綠色嘅蝴蝶，好細隻嘅，大確一吋咁上下嘅一隻蝴蝶，「僕」咗喺我件衫度。我本來想用手拍佢走，但係唔知點解我覺得……好似唔應該用手拍佢，跟住就細細力將件外套一「等」，將佢「等」走，就趕上病房。行咗幾步……我停落嚟……「爸爸，佢係爸爸，佢要跟住我嚟……佢要我帶佢上去搵阿媽？……佢嚟接阿媽走？」……我就拎返轉頭望出去，想睇吓隻蝴蝶仲喺唔喺度，不過已經見唔倒。

大確中午阿媽開始呼吸愈嚟愈困難。我諗起隻蝴蝶。阿媽仲未走……係咪因為老豆蕩失路呢？我頭先應該由佢喺我件衫度咪好囉。兩點鐘左右我落樓下搵嗰隻蝴蝶，我怕佢真係蕩失路，但係搵唔倒。我就上病房，我一路上樓梯……一路諗住老竇嗰件恤衫……

（*寬身上的燈暗。*）

（*此場完。*）

KUAN   Almost seven hours. That day, we watched
            her at the hospital for seven hours. Sister, her
            husband, their daughter, we were all by her
            bed watching her. We did nothing else. We just
            held her hand and watched her. Sometimes I
            thought to myself, does she know we're here?
            Is she in pain? ... So we stayed with her at the
            hospital for the last seven hours.

            (Pause.)

KUAN   One more thing. That morning when we arrived
            at the hospital, when we got to the elevator,
            Sister stopped me, "Wait, there's a bug on
            your back." I stopped and carefully took off
            my jacket to look. It was a pale green butterfly.
            Very small. About one inch or so. It was on my
            jacket. I wanted to brush it away with my hand,
            but for some reason I felt... I shouldn't brush it
            away. Then I just gently shook my jacket, shook
            it off, and hurried up to the ward. I walked a
            few steps... I stopped... "Dad, it was dad. He
            followed me... Does he want me to take him
            upstairs to find mom?... Has he come for her?"
            I turned around to see if the butterfly was still
            there, but it was gone.

            Mom began to have trouble breathing around
            noon. I thought about the butterfly. Mom was
            still there... was it because dad had lost his
            way? I should have left him on my jacket.
            Around two o'clock, I went downstairs to look
            for the butterfly. I was afraid it might be lost.
            But I couldn't find it. So I returned to the ward.
            On the way upstairs, I thought about dad's
            shirt.

            (The light on Kuan dims.)

            (End of scene.)

尾聲

（*天空中出現閃耀的星星，演員看著天上的星星。明亮的燈光慢慢地照亮整個劇場，演員站在台上看著觀眾席。*）

（*燈暗。*）

全劇完

EPILOGUE

(Stars sparkle in the sky. The actors look at the stars. The lights slowly light up the entire stage. The actors stand on the stage and look at the audience.)

(Lights dim.)

The End.

The Hong Kong Arts Festival

The Hong Kong Arts Festival, established in 1972, presents close to 150 performances and events by top international, regional, national and local talent during February and March each year. The eclectic mix of classical and contemporary works cater to an audience of about 120,000 including participants of the Festival's Young Friends Scheme. The Festival also commissions, produces and publishes new works independently or in collaboration with international partners. Festival information is available at www.hk.artsfestival.org.

香港藝術節簡介

香港藝術節成立於1972年,為國際藝壇重要的表演藝術節之一。多年來已邀請接近150個本地、亞洲及世界頂尖藝人及團隊到藝術節表演。藝術節的節目式式俱備,既顧及古典傳統口味,亦具備創意新奇和香港難得一見的表演形式,每屆入場觀眾人次達十二萬。近年,藝術節與亞洲區內其他藝術節積極合作,孕育新作,與國際上重要藝術機構聯合委約新創作,並支持不同領域的藝術家進行跨區跨媒體的合作。此外,香港藝術節「青少年之友」計劃,致力培養年青人對藝術的興趣,過去十八年間已有超過五十八萬個中學及大學生參與。經過三十八年的發展,今天的藝術節不論在表演藝人數目、演出水平、節目種類各方面,均為本地藝壇之最。

香港藝術節
Hong Kong Arts Festival

督印人 Publisher	何嘉坤 Tisa Ho
主編 Editor	蘇國雲 / 方博德 So Kwok-wan / Frank Proctor
編輯審校 Executive Editor	梁偉然 Ian Leung
平面設計 排版 Designer	楚 翹 Devorah Jowie Chan
攝影 Photographers	梁栢康 Patrick Leung
協助 Coordinator	蘇泳琪 So Wing Kei
出版 Published by	香港藝術節協會有限公司 Hong Kong Arts Festival Society Limited
印刷 Printer	雅聯印刷有限公司 Allion Printing Limited
版次 Edition	2011年3月初版 1st edition in March 2011
書號/ISBN	978-988-18176-6-2
定價/Price	港幣HK$80
版權垂詢: Copyright Enquiry	香港藝術節協會有限公司 Hong Kong Arts Festival Society Limited 香港灣仔港灣道二號12字樓 12/F, 2 Harbour Road, Wan Chai, Hong Kong 電話Tel: 2824 3555 傳真Fax: 2824 3798, 2824 3722 網頁Website: www.hk.artsfestival.org 電郵Email: afgen@hkaf.org